CU00660830

T
LOVELINESS
OF CHRIST

SAMUEL RUTHERFORD

SELECTED BY ELLEN LISTER

PREFATORY NOTE BY BISHOP HANDLEY DUNELM

VINTAGE PURITAN SERIES
GLH PUBLISHING
Louisville, Kentucky

Originally Published in 1909.
Public Domain

Footnotes have been included to aid the reader.
Footnotes © GLH Publishing, 2016

ISBN:
  Paperback 978-1-941129-39-5

CONTENTS

Prefatory Note 1
Preface 2
Brief Selections from the Letters of Samuel
    Rutherford 6
To Mistress Taylor 38
To the Lady Earlstoun 41
For Marion M'Knaught 42

Prefatory Note

By the Bishop of Durham

This book, a small casket stored with many jewels, will have, I hope, a wide circulation. Yet more I hope that it will go deep as well as far, and imprint by the grace of God upon an its readers' souls something of that supreme content and delight in the Lord Jesus which were the light of the life to Samuel Rutherford. Nothing is more needed in our day in the Christian Church than a larger sight by faith, of "the King in His beauty." We hear much of many things, but too little of Him.

To read Rutherford, in sympathy and with prayer, is a powerful and beautiful help towards that "beatific vision" of our Redeemer which may be ours even here below.

Handley Dunelm

PREFACE

Samuel Rutherford, the author of the famous "Letters," was born at the Tillage of Nisbet in Roxburghshire in 1600, seven years after the birth of George Herbert, and eight before that of John Milton, and was contemporary with Shakespeare. He was educated at Jedburgh, and entered Edinburgh University in 1617. There he took his degree of Master of Arts in 1621, and obtained the appointment of Professor of Humanity soon after. Little is known of him till, at the age of twenty-seven, he became minister of the small parish of Anwoth, on the Solway. Here he laboured diligently for nine years, among a poor and ignorant people, "the whole country coming to him and accounting themselves as his particular flock." A contemporary minister said of him, "He seemed to be always praying, always preaching, always visiting the sick, always catechising, always writing and studying. He had two quick eyes, and when he walked it was observed that he held *aye his face upward*. He had a strange utterance in the pulpit—a kind of *skreigh*[1] that I never heard the like. Many times I thought he would have flown out of the pulpit when he came to speak of Jesus Christ. He was never in his right element but when he was commending Him."

The oft-told story of the visit paid him by Archbishop Usher belongs to this period of his life.

"The Archbishop, when passing through Galloway, was anxious to meet with Rutherford, of whose piety he heard much, and better to accomplish his purpose, he appeared at the manse,[2] on a Saturday evening, in the

---

1 Screech, abrupt scream.
2 Parsonage.

disguise of mendicant.[3] Mrs. Rutherford, according to custom, called the servants together for examination preparatory to the solemnities of the Sabbath, and the stranger took his place among them. In the course of examination he was asked, 'How many commandments are there?' 'Eleven,' was the reply. On receiving this answer, the good lady replied, 'What a shame is it for you, a man with grey hairs, in a Christian country, not to know how many commandments there are! There is not a child of six years old in the parish but could answer this question properly.' She troubled the poor man no more, thinking him so very ignorant, but lamented his condition to the servants, and after giving him some supper, desired a servant to show him upstairs, to a bed in the garret.[4] Rutherford repaired early in the morning, as usual, to a favourite walk near the manse, for meditation, and was startled on hearing the voice of prayer, proceeding from a thicket, earnestly imploring a blessing on behalf of the people that day to assemble. Rutherford began to think that he had 'entertained angels unawares.' An explanation followed, and Rutherford requested him to preach that day to his people, which the Archbishop agreed to do, on condition that he would not discover him to any other. Mrs. Rutherford found that the poor man had gone away before any of the family were out of bed. Rutherford presented him with a suit of his own clothes, and introduced him as a strange minister passing by, who had promised to preach for him. After domestic worship and breakfast, the family went to church; and Usher had for his text, John xiii. 34, 'A new commandment I give unto you, that ye love one another.' In the course of his sermon, he observed that that might be reckoned the eleventh commandment, upon which Mrs. Rutherford said to herself, 'That is the answer the poor man gave me last night;' and looking up to the pulpit said, 'It cannot be possible that this is he!' He returned with Rutherford to the manse, an evening was

---

3   Pauper, beggar.

4   Attic, loft.

spent together with mutual pleasure and profit."

In July 1636 Rutherford was summoned to appear before the High Commission Court to answer for his Nonconformity to the Acts of Episcopacy, and also on account of his treatise against the Arminians; and as a consequence was forbidden to exercise his ministry anywhere in the kingdom of Scotland, and to confine himself to the city of Aberdeen. It was while confined to this place that the greater portion of his "Letters" were written. Richard Baxter's opinion of these is well worth quoting: "Hold off the Bible; such a book the world never saw." In 1638 events had taken a more favourable turn for the cause of the Reformation in Scotland, and Rutherford returned to his people at Anwoth for a time; but in 1639 he was removed to the Professor's chair and made Principal of the New College in St. Andrews. At the same time he was colleague in the ministry with Mr. Blair in that city. Of the fruit of his labours there, M'Ward, his old editor, who knew him well, says: "God did so singularly second His servant's indefatigable pains, both in teaching in the school and preaching in the congregation, that it became forthwith a Lebanon out of which were taken cedars for building the house of the Lord through the whole land."

An English merchant who heard him preach in St. Andrews says: "I went to St. Andrews, where I heard a sweet majestic-looking man (Blair), and he showed me *the majesty of God*. After him a little fair man (Rutherford), and he showed me *the loveliness of Christ*."

Rutherford was one of the commissioners sent up by the Church of Scotland to the Westminster Assembly in 1643, and he took a prominent part.

His celebrated work, *Lex Rex*, was so hateful to the Government that shortly before his death they ordered it to be burned in Edinburgh by the common hangman. When on his death-bed he was summoned to appear at Edinburgh on a charge of high treason, and had it been his Master's will, he would joyfully have met a martyr's death. On March 20, 1661, he entered into rest at St. Andrews, and was buried there.

From a well-marked, much-loved copy of his "Letters" these selections have been made. Strong and quaint and bracing are the words of this saint of olden time—very unlike the feeble wails we often hear in these days. People seem now to consider it more than *unfair* to have to bear the weakest cross, and certainly not to "count it all joy" with St. James. With prayer and hope this little book has come down to us through the centuries concerning "the loveliness of Christ."

BRIEF SELECTIONS FROM THE LETTERS OF SAMUEL RUTHERFORD

The great Master Gardener, the Father of our Lord Jesus Christ, in a wonderful providence, with His own hand, planted me here, where by His grace, in this part of His vineyard, I grow; and here I will abide till the great Master of the vineyard think fit to transplant me.

If your Lord call you to suffering, be not dismayed; there shall be a new allowance of the King for you when ye come to it. One of the softest pillows Christ hath is laid under His witnesses' head, though often they must set down their bare feet among thorns.

God hath called you to Christ's side, and the wind is now in Christ's face in this land; and seeing ye are with Him, ye cannot expect the lee-side or the sunny side of the brae.[5]

He delighteth to take up fallen bairns[6] and to mend broken brows: binding up of wounds is His office.

Wants are my best riches, for I have these supplied by Christ.

I hope to over-hope and over-believe my troubles.

I think the sense of our wants, when withal we have a restlessness and a sort of spiritual impatience under them, and can make a din, because we want Him whom

---

5   Slope of a hill.
6   Children.

our soul loveth, is that which maketh an open door to Christ: and when we think we are going backward, because we feel deadness, we are going forward; for the more sense the more life, and no sense argueth no life.

There is no sweeter fellowship with Christ than to bring our wounds and our sores to Him.

There is as much in our Lord's pantry as will satisfy all His bairns, and as much wine in His cellar as will quench all their thirst. Hunger on; for there is meat in hunger for Christ: go never from Him, but fash[7] Him (who yet is pleased with the importunity of hungry souls) with a dishful of hungry desires, till He fill you; and if He delay yet come not ye away, albeit ye should fall a-swoon at His feet.

I find it most true, that the greatest temptation out of hell, is to live without temptations; if my waters should stand, they would rot. Faith is the better of the free air, and of the sharp winter storm in its face. Grace withereth without adversity. The devil is but God's master fencer, to teach us to handle our weapons.

O, pity for evermore that there should be such an one as Christ Jesus, so boundless, so bottomless, and so incomparable in infinite excellency, and sweetness, and so few to take Him! O, ye poor dry dead souls, why will ye not come hither with your toom[8] vessels and your empty souls to this huge, and fair, and deep, and sweet well of life, and fill all your toom vessels?

O, that Christ should be so large in sweetness and worth, and we so narrow, pinched, so ebb,[9] and so void of all happiness, and yet men will not take Him! they lose their love miserably, who will not bestow it upon this lovely One.

I know all created power should sink under me if I

---

7   Pester, bother.

8   Empty.

9   Shallow, decaying.

should lean down upon it, and therefore it is better to rest on God than sink or fall; and we weak souls must have a bottom and being-place, for we cannot stand out alone. Let us then be wise in our choice and choose and wail our own blessedness, which is to trust in the Lord.

They are not lost to you that are laid up in Christ's treasury in heaven.

At the resurrection ye shall meet with them: there they are, sent before but not sent away. Your Lord loveth you, who is homely to take and give, borrow and lend.

Ye will not get leave to steal quietly to heaven, in Christ's company, without a conflict and a cross.

I find crosses Christ's carved work that He marketh out for us, and that with crosses He figureth and portrayeth us to His own image, cutting away pieces of our ill and corruption. Lord cut, Lord carve, Lord wound, Lord do anything that may perfect Thy Father's image in us, and make us meet for glory.

It is the Lord's kindness that He will take the scum off us in the fire. Who knoweth how needful winnowing is to us, and what dross we must want ere we enter into the kingdom of God? So narrow is the entry to heaven, that our knots, our bunches and lumps of pride, and self-love, and idol-love, and world-love must be hammered off us, that we may throng in, stooping low, and creeping through that narrow and thorny entry.

O, what owe I to the file, to the hammer, to the furnace of my Lord Jesus!

Why should I start at the plough of my Lord, that maketh deep furrows on my soul? I know He is no idle husbandman, He purposeth a crop.

Crosses are proclaimed as common accidents to all the saints, and in them standeth a part of our communion with Christ.

How sweet a thing were it for us to learn to make our burdens light by framing our hearts to the burden, and making our Lord's will a law.

It is not the sunny side of Christ that we must look to, and we must not forsake Him for want of that; but must set our face against what may befall us, in following on, till He and we through the briers and bushes on the dry ground. Our soft nature would be borne through the troubles of this miserable life in Christ's arms. And it is His wisdom, who knoweth our mould, that His bairns go wet-shod and cold-footed to heaven.

There is nothing but perfect garden-flowers in heaven, and the best plenishing[10] that is there is Christ.

It is not a smooth and easy way, neither will your weather be fair and pleasant; but whosoever saw the invisible God and the fair city, makes no reckoning of losses or crosses. In ye must be, cost you what it will; stand not for a price, and for all that ye have, to win the castle; the rights of it are won to you, and it is disponed[11] to you, in your Lord Jesus' Testament; and see what a fair legacy your dying Friend, Christ, hath left you: and there wanteth nothing but possession.

O! men's souls have no wings, and therefore night and day they keep their nest and are not acquaint with Christ.

> What can I say of Him?
> Let us go and see.

I have little, little of Him; yet I long for more.

Scar[12] not at suffering for Christ: for Christ hath a chair, and a cushion, and sweet peace for a sufferer.

He taketh the bairns in His arms when they come to a deep water; at least, when they lose ground, and are put

---

10 Stock.

11 Dispose of property in one's will.

12 To be scared, frightened.

to swim, then His hand is under their chin.

My shallow and ebb thoughts are not the compass Christ saileth by. I leave His ways to Himself, for they are far, far above me.…There are windings and to's and fro's in His ways, which blind bodies like us cannot see.

I see grace groweth best in winter.

I know, we may say, that Christ is kindest in His love when we are at our weakest; and that if Christ had not been to the fore, in our sad days, the waters had gone over our soul.

I verily judge, we know not how much may be had in this life: there is yet something beyond all we see, that seeking would light upon.

Let Him make anything out of me, so being He be glorified in my salvation: for I know I am made for Him.

Men do lop the branches off their trees round about, to the end they may grow up high and tall. The Lord hath this way lopped your branch, in taking from you many children, to the end ye should grow upward, like one of the Lord's cedars.

Poor folks must either borrow or beg from the rich, and the only thing that commendeth sinners to Christ is extreme necessity and want. Christ's love is ready to make and provide a ransom and money for a poor body who hath lost his purse. "Ho, ye that have no money, come and buy" (Isaiah lv. 1). That is the poor man's market.

Every day we may see some new thing in Christ. His love hath neither brim nor bottom.

Go where ye will, your soul shall not sleep sound but in Christ's bosom.

I find that our wants qualify us for Christ.

My dear brother, I will think it comfort if ye speak my

name to our Well-Beloved wherever you are. I am mindful of you.

I bless you for your prayers; add to them praises. As I am able, I pay you home.

Blessed were we if we could make ourselves masters of that invaluable treasure, the love of Christ; or rather suffer ourselves to be mastered and subdued to Christ's love, so as Christ were our all things, and all others things our nothings, and the refuse of our delights. O, let us be ready for shipping against the time our Lord's wind and tide call for us.

There are infinite plies in His love that the saints will never win to unfold.

When I look over beyond the line and beyond death, to the laughing side of the world, I triumph, and ride upon the high places of Jacob: howbeit, otherways I am a faint, deadhearted, cowardly man, oft borne down and hungry in waiting for the marriage supper of the Lamb.

Nevertheless, I think it the Lord's wise love that feeds us with hunger, and makes us fat with wants and desertion.

It is little up or little down that the Lamb and His followers can get, no law-surety nor truce with crosses;[13] it must be so till we are up in our Father's house.

I urge upon you…a nearer communion with Christ and a growing communion. There are curtains to be drawn by in Christ that we never saw, and new foldings of love in Him. I despair that ever I shall win to the far end of that love, there are so many plies in it; therefore dig deep, and sweat, and labour, and take pains for Him, and set by so much time in the day for Him as you can: He will be won with labour.

Neither need we fear crosses, or sigh, or be sad for any-

---

13   Not to expect or receive promise of peace or experience no trials.

thing that is on this side of heaven, if we have Christ.

O, that we could put our treasure in Christ's hand, and give Him our gold to keep, and our crown.

Our fair morning is at hand, the day-star is near the rising, and we are not many miles from home; what matters the ill entertainment in the smoky inns of this miserable life? We are not to stay here, and we will be dearly welcome to Him whom we go to.

Be patient; Christ went to Heaven with many a wrong. His visage and countenance was all marred more than the sons of men. You may not be above your Master; many a black stroke received innocent Jesus, and He received no mends, but referred them all to the great court-day, when all things shall be righted.

Out of whatever airt[14] the wind blow, it will blow us on our Lord: no wind can blow our sails overboard, because Christ's skill and the honour of His wisdom are empawned[15] and laid down at the stake for the sea-passengers, that He shall put them safe off His hand on the shore, in His Father's known bounds, our native home ground.

It is impossible to be submissive and religiously patient, if ye stay your thoughts down among the confused rollings and wheels of second causes, as O, the place! O, the time! O, if this had been, this had not followed! O, the linking of this accident with this time and place! Look up to the master motion and the first wheel.

God hath made many fair flowers, but the fairest of them all is heaven, and the flower of all flowers is Christ.

When we shall come home and enter to the possession of our Brother's fair kingdom, and when our heads shall find the weight of the eternal crown of glory, and when

---

14 Direction.

15 Pledged.

we shall look back to pains and sufferings; then shall we see life and sorrow to be less than one step or stride from a prison to glory; and that our little inch of time-suffering is not worthy of our first night's welcome home to heaven.

We smell of the smoke of this lower house of the earth, because our hearts and our thoughts are here. If we could mount up with God, we should smell of heaven and of our country above, and we should look like our country, and like strangers or people not born or brought up here-away.[16] Our crosses would not bite upon us, if we were heavenly minded.

Lay all your loads and your weights by faith upon Christ. Ease yourself, and let Him bear all. He can, He does, He will bear you.

Our best fare here is hunger.

This world deserveth nothing but the outer court of our soul.

I think I see more of Christ than ever I saw; and yet I see but little of what may be seen.

Christ's cross is such a burden as sails are to a ship or wings to a bird.

Whether God come to His children with a rod or a crown, if He come Himself with it, it is well. Welcome, welcome Jesus, what way soever Thou come, if we can get a sight of Thee: and sure I am, it is better to be sick, providing Christ come to the bedside and draw the curtains, and say, Courage, I am thy salvation, than to enjoy health being lusty and strong and never to be visited by God.

There are many heads lying in Christ's bosom, but here is room for yours among the rest.

I am half content to have boils for my Lord Jesus's plais-

---

16 Hereabouts.

ters.[17] Sickness hath this advantage, that it draweth our sweet Physician's hand and His holy and soft fingers to touch our withered and leper skins: it is a blessed fever that fetcheth Christ to the bedside—I think my Lord's, "How doest thou with it, sick body?" is worth all my pained nights.

It is our heaven to lay many weights and burdens upon Christ.

Let Him find much employment for His calling with you; for He is such a Friend as delighteth to be burdened with suits and employments; and the more ye lay on Him, and the more homely ye be with Him, the more welcome.

Our love to Him should begin on earth, as it shall be in heaven; for the bride taketh not by a thousand degrees so much delight in her wedding garment as she doth in her bridegroom; so we, in the life to come, howbeit clothed with glory as with a robe, shall not be so much affected with the glory that goeth about us, as with the Bridegroom's joyful face and presence.

I hope ye are not ignorant, that if peace was left to you in Christ's testament, so the other half of the testament was a legacy of Christ's sufferings. John xvi. 33.

His winds turn not when He seemeth to change, it is but we who turn our wrong side to Him.

I am like a low man looking up to a high mountain, whom weariness and fainting overcometh. I would climb up, but I find that I do not advance in my journey as I would wish: yet I trust He shall take me home against night.

I think it a sweet thing, that Christ saith of my cross, half mine, and that He divideth these sufferings with me and taketh the largest share to Himself; nay, that I, and my

---

17   Dressing or bandage for a wound.

whole cross, are wholly Christ's.

Live on Christ's love while ye are here, and all the way.

Faith is exceeding charitable, and believeth no evil of God.

You must learn to make evils your great good, and to spin out comforts, peace, joy, communion with Christ, out of your troubles, that are Christ's wooers to speak for you to Himself.

Christ's love, under a vail[18] is love; if ye get Christ, how-beit not the sweet and pleasant way you would have Him, it is enough, for the Well-Beloved cometh not our way.

Put Christ's love to the trial and put upon it burdens, and then it will appear love indeed.

Your rock doth not ebb and flow, but your sea.

The sea-sick passenger shall come to land; Christ will be the first that will meet you on the shore.

Faith liveth and spendeth upon our Captain's charges, who is able to pay for all.

Christ is as full a feast, as ye can have to hunger.

Our Lord hunteth for our love, more ways than one or two.

Christ hath come, and run away to heaven with my heart and my love, so that neither heart nor love is mine.

I see Christ's love is so kingly, that it will not abide a marrow:[19] it must have a throne all alone in the soul.

The child hath but changed a bed in the garden, and is planted up higher, nearer the sun, where he shall thrive

---

18   Veil.

19   A partner, an equal associate.

better than in this out-field moor-ground.

Go on, and faint not, something of yours is in heaven, beside the flesh of your exalted Saviour, and ye go on after your own.

He is not lost to you who is found to Christ. If he hath casten[20] his bloom and flower, the bloom is fallen in heaven in Christ's lap; and as he was lent awhile to time, so is he given now to eternity, which will take yourself; and the difference of your shipping and his to heaven and Christ's shore, the land of life, is only in some few years, which weareth every day shorter, and some short and soon reckoned summers will give you a meeting with him.

I pray you learn to be worthy of His pains who correcteth; and let Him wring, and be ye washed; for He hath a Father's heart, and a Father's hand, who is training you up, and making you meet for the high hall.

One year's time of heaven shall swallow up all sorrows, even beyond all comparison.

Fall down and make a surrender of those that are gone, and these that are yet alive, to Him. And for you, let Him have all; and wait for Himself, for He will come and will not tarry. Live by faith…He cannot die whose ye are.

I beseech you in the Lord Jesus, to make every day more and more of Christ, and try your growth in the grace of God, and what ground ye win daily on corruption; for travellers are day by day, either advancing farther on, and nearer home, or else they go not right about to compass their journey.

It will not fail you to get two portions, and to laugh twice, and to be happy twice, and to have an upper heaven, and an under heaven too; Christ our Lord and His saints were not so, and therefore let go your grip of

---

20   Cast, shed, dropped.

this life and of the good things of it. I hope your heaven groweth not hereaway.[21] Learn daily both to possess and miss Christ in His secret Bridegroom smiles; He must go and come, because His infinite wisdom thinketh it best for you. We will be together one day; we shall not need to borrow light from sun, moon, or candle; there shall be no complaints on either side in heaven; there shall be none there but He and we, the Bridegroom and the bride; devils, temptations, trials, desertions, losses, sad hearts, pain, and death, shall all be put out of play, and the devil must give up his office of tempting. O, blessed is the soul whose hope hath a face looking straight out to that day.

It is our folly to divide our narrow and little love. It will not serve two; best then hold it whole and together, and give it to Christ! for then, we get double interest for our love, when we lend it to and lay it out upon Christ; and we are sure besides that the stock cannot perish.

She is not sent away, but only sent before, like unto a star, which, going out of your sight, doth not die and vanish, but shineth in another hemisphere: ye see her not yet, she doth shine in another country.

Ye are now your alone, but ye may have for the seeking, three always in your company, the Father, Son, and Holy Spirit; I trust they are near you.

If contentment were here, heaven were not heaven.

Read and spell right, for He knoweth what He doth; He is only lopping and snedding[22] a fruitful tree, that it may be more fruitful.

Do that for the Lord which ye will do for time; time will calm your heart at that which God hath done, and let our Lord have it now. What love ye did bear to friends now dead, seeing they stand now in no need of it, let it fall as

---

21 Hereabouts, near or around this place.

22 Cut, trim, prune.

just legacy to Christ.

Put Christ in His own room in your love; it may be He hath either been out of His own place, or in a place of love inferior to His worth.

I wonder many times that ever a child of God should have a sad heart, considering what their Lord is preparing for them.

Send a heavy heart up to Christ, it shall be welcome.

I am persuaded, Christ is responsal[23] and law-abiding, to make recompense for anything that is hazarded or given out for Him; losses for Christ are but our goods given out in bank[24] in Christ's hand.

I bless the Lord, that all our troubles come through Christ's fingers, and that He casteth sugar among them; and casteth in some ounce weights of heaven and of the spirit of glory in our cup.

Take no heavier lift of your children, than your Lord alloweth; give them room beside your heart, but not in the yolk of your heart, where Christ should be; for then they are your idols, not your bairns. If your Lord take any of them home to His house before the storm come on, take it well, the Owner of the orchard may take down two or three apples off His own trees, before midsummer, and ere they get the harvest sun; and it would not be seemly that His servant, the gardener, should chide Him for it. Let our Lord pluck His own fruit at any season He pleaseth; they are not lost to you, they are laid up so well, as that they are coffered in heaven, where our Lord's best jewels lie.

Let Christ have a commanding power and a King-throne in you.

23　Answerable, responsible.

24　As a loan.

I find His sweet presence eateth out the bitterness of sorrow and suffering.

To live on Christ's love is a king's life.

If I come to heaven any way, howbeit like a tired traveller upon my Guide's shoulder, it is good enough for those who have no legs of their own for such a journey. I never thought there had been need of so much wrestling to win to the top of that steep mountain as now I find.

Go up beforehand and see your lodging. Look through all your Father's rooms in heaven; in your Father's house are many dwelling-places. Men take a sight of lands ere they buy them. I know Christ hath made the bargain already: but be kind to the house you are going to, and see it often.

All the saints have their own measure of winter before their eternal summer. O! for the long day, and the high sun, and the fair garden, and the King's great city up above these visible heavens! What God layeth on, let us suffer, for some have one cross, some seven, some ten, some half a cross—yet all the saints have whole and full joy, and seven crosses have seven joys.

Glorify the Lord in your sufferings, and take His banner of love, and spread it over you. Others will follow you, if they see you strong in the Lord; their courage shall take life from your Christian carriage.

The weightiest end of the cross of Christ that is laid upon you, lieth upon your strong Saviour.

O, if I could be master of that house-idol myself, my own, mine, my own will, wit, credit, and ease, how blessed were I! O, but we have need to be redeemed from ourselves rather than from the devil and the world; learn to put out yourselves, and to put in Christ for yourselves.

Christ all the seasons of the year, is dropping sweetness;

if I had vessels I might fill them, but my old riven,[25] hol-ey, and running-out dish, even when I am at the well, can bring little away. Nothing but glory will make tight and fast our leaking and rifty[26] vessels....How little of the sea can a child carry in his hand; as little do I take away of my great sea, my boundless and running-over Christ Jesus.

Sure I am He is the far best half of heaven; yea He is all heaven, and more than all heaven.

Ye may yourself ebb and flow, rise and fall, wax and wane; but your Lord is this day as He was yesterday; and it is your comfort that your salvation is not rolled upon wheels of your own making, neither have ye to do with a Christ of your own shaping.

Put your hand to the pen, and let the cross of your Lord Jesus have your submissive and resolute Amen.

The floods may swell and roar, but our ark shall swim above the waters; it cannot sink, because a Saviour is in it.

Let not salvation be your by-work,[27] or your holiday's task only, or a work by the way: for men think, that this may be done in three days' space on a feather-bed, when death and they are fallen in hands together, and that with a word or two they shall make their soul matters right. Alas, this is to sit loose and unsure in the matters of our salvation.

How soon will some few years pass away, and then when the day is ended, and this life's lease expired, what have men of the world's glory, but dreams and thoughts? O happy soul for evermore, who can rightly compare this life with that long-lasting life to come, and can balance the weighty glory of the one with the light golden vanity of the other.

---

25 Split.

26 Splitting.

27 Work done on the side, work done in one's spare time.

Lay no more on the creatures than they are able to carry. Lay your soul and your weights upon God; make Him your only, only best Beloved—your errand in this life is to make sure an eternity of glory to your soul, and to match your soul with Christ; your love, if it were more than all the love of angels in one, is Christ's due.…I know not what ye have if ye want Christ.

It is not our part to make a treasure here: anything under the covering of heaven we can build upon, is but ill ground and a sandy foundation: every good thing, except God, wanteth a bottom, and cannot stand its alone: how then can it bear the weight of us?

I would wish each cross were looked in the face seven times, and were read over and over again. It is the messenger of the Lord and speaks something.

Try what is the taste of the Lord's cup and drink with God's blessing, that ye may grow thereby. I trust in God, whatever other speech it utter to your soul, this is one word in it, "Behold, blessed is the man whom God correcteth." And that it saith to you, ye are from home while here, ye are not of this world, as your Redeemer Christ was not of this world. There is something keeping for you which is worth the having. All that is here is condemned to die—to pass away like a snow-ball before a summer sun; and since death took first possession of something of yours, it hath been and daily is creeping nearer and nearer to yourself, howbeit with no noise of feet. Your Husbandman and Lord hath lopped off some branches already, the tree itself is to be transplanted to the high garden. All these crosses are to make you white and ripe for the Lord's harvest hook.

What is His purpose herein, He knoweth best who hath taken your soul in tutoring. Your faith may be boldly charitable of Christ, that however matters go, the worst shall be a tired traveller, and a joyful and sweet welcome home: the back of your winter night is broken. Look to the East—the day sky is breaking; think not that Christ loseth time or lingereth unsuitably.

If Christ Jesus be the period, the end and lodging-home, at the end of your journey, there is no fear, ye go to a friend…ye may look death in the face with joy.

O wretched idol, myself! when shall I see thee wholly decourted,[28] and Christ wholly put in thy room? O, if Christ, Christ, had the full place and room of myself, that all my aims, purposes, thoughts, and desires, would coast and land upon Christ, and not upon myself! And yet, howbeit we cannot attain to this denial of me and mine that we can say I am not myself, myself is not myself, mine own is no longer my own; yet our aiming at this in all we do shall be accepted; for, alas, I think I shall die but minting and aiming to be a Christian.

I am sure the saints at their best are but strangers to the weight and worth of the incomparable sweetness of Christ. He is so new, so fresh in excellency, every day of new, to these that search more and more in Him, as if Heaven could furnish as many new Christs (if I may speak so) as there are days betwixt Him and us, and yet He is one and the same.

O, we love an unknown lover when we love Christ.

I thought it had been an easy thing to be a Christian, and that to seek God had been at the next door, but oh, the windings, the turnings, the ups and the downs that He hath led me through! and I see yet much way to the ford.

O, what need have I to have the ashes blown away from my dying-out fire! I may be a book-man, and be an idiot and stark fool in Christ's way; learning will not beguile Christ: the Bible beguiled the Pharisees, and so may I be misted.[29] Therefore, as night-watchers hold one another waking by speaking to one another, so have we need to hold one another on foot.

Be not afraid for little grace. Christ soweth His living seed, and He will not lose His seed; if He have the guid-

---

28   Dismiss or banish from the court.

29   Obsured, dimmed, mistaken.

ing of my stock and state it shall not miscarry. Our spilt works, losses, deadness, coldness, wretchedness, are the ground which the good Husbandman laboureth.

I have heard a rumour of the prelate's purpose to banish me, but let it come if God so will; the other side of the sea is my Father's ground as well as this side.

Look up to Him and love Him! O, love and live.

Our pride must have winter weather to rot it.

He hath made all His promises good to me and hath filled up all the blanks with His own hand.

I dare not say but my Lord Jesus hath fully recompensed my sadness with His joys, my losses with His own presence. I find it a sweet and rich thing to exchange my sorrows with Christ's joys, my afflictions with that sweet peace I have with Himself.

Providence hath a thousand keys to open a thousand sundry doors for the deliverance of His own, when it is even come to a *conclamatum est*.[30] Let us be faithful and care for our own part, which is to do and suffer for Him, and lay Christ's part on Himself, and leave it there; duties are ours, events are the Lord's.

Temptations will come, but if they be not made welcome by you, ye have the best of it; be jealous over yourself, and your own heart, and keep touches with God; let Him not have a faint and feeble soldier of you; fear not to back Christ, for He will conquer and over more; let no man scar at Christ, for I have no quarrels at His cross. He and His cross are two good guests, and worth the lodging. Men would fain have Christ good cheap, but the mercat[31] will not come down. Acquaint yourself with prayer, make Christ your Captain and your Armour; make conscience of sinning when no eye seeth you.

---

30   "It is all over."

31   Market price.

He cutteth off your love to the creature, that ye might learn that God only is the right owner of your love, sorrow, loss, sadness, death or the worst things that are, except sin: but Christ knoweth well what to make of them, and can put His own in the crosses common, that we shall be obliged to affliction, and thank God, who learned us to make our acquaintance with such a rough companion, who can hale[32] us to Christ.

It is easy to get good words and a comfortable message from our Lord, even from such rough sergeants as diverse temptations.

Let us be glad and rejoice in the salvation of our Lord, for faith had never yet cause to have wet cheeks and hanging-down brows, or to droop or die; what can ail faith, seeing Christ suffereth Himself (with reverence to Him be it spoken) to be commanded by it; and Christ commandeth all things. Faith may dance because Christ sings; and we may come in the quire[33] and lift our hoarse and rough voices, and chirp, and sing, and shout for joy with our Lord Jesus.

None have right to joy but we, for joy is sown for us, and an ill summer or harvest will not spill[34] the crop.

Christ and His cross together are sweet company, and a blessed couple. My prison is my palace, my losses are rich losses, my pain easy pain, my heavy days are holy and happy days. I may tell a new tale of Christ to my friends.

I know my Lord is no niggard:[35] He can, and it becometh Him well to give more than my narrow soul can receive.
 If there were ten thousand, thousand millions of worlds, and as many heavens full of men and angels, Christ would not be pinched to supply all our wants,

---

32 Compel, haul, pull.

33 Choir.

34 Destroy.

35 A stingy or ungenerous person.

and to fill us all.

Christ is a well of life, but who knoweth how deep it is to the bottom?

This soul of ours hath love, and cannot but love some fair one; and O, what a fair One, what an only One, what an excellent, lovely, ravishing One is Jesus.

O, come all and drink at this living well; come, drink, and live for evermore; come, drink, and welcome; welcome, saith our fairest Bridegroom: no man getteth Christ with ill will: no man cometh and is not welcome, no man cometh and rueth[36] his voyage: all men speak well of Christ, who have been at Him; men and angels who know Him will say more than I now do, and think more of Him than they can say.

It should be enough to me, if I were wise, that Christ will have joy and sorrow halfers[37] of the life of the saints, and that each of them should have a share of our days, as the night and the day are kindly partners and halfers of time and take it up betwixt them. But if sorrow be the greediest halfer of our days here, I know joy's day shall dawn, and do more than recompense all our sad hours.

I am in this house of my pilgrimage every way in good case; Christ is most kind and loving to my soul: it pleaseth Him to feast with his unseen consolations a stranger, and an exiled prisoner: and I would not exchange my Lord Jesus, with all the comfort out of heaven; His yoke is easy, and His burden light. This is His truth I now suffer for; for He hath sealed it with His blessed presence.

Happy are they who are found watching. Our sand-glass is not so long as we need to weary: time will eat away and root out our woes and sorrow: our heaven is in the bud, and growing up to an harvest; why then should we not follow on, seeing our span-length of time will come to an inch? Therefore I commend Christ to you as the

---

36 Be sorrow for, regrets.

37 Half of.

Staff of your old age: let Him have now the rest of your days; and think not much of a storm upon the ship that Christ saileth in; there shall no passenger fall overboard; but the crazed[38] ship and the sea-sick passenger shall come to land safe.

I am in as sweet communion with Christ as a poor sinner can be; and am only pained that He hath much beauty and fairness, and I little love; He great power and mercy, and I little faith; He much light, and I bleared eyes.

My counsel is, that ye come out and leave the multitude, and let Christ have your company. Let them take clay and this present world who love it: Christ is a more worthy and noble portion: blessed are those who get Him.

My dear brother, let God make of you what He will, He will end all with consolation, and shall make glory out of your sufferings; and would ye wish better work?

This water was in your way to heaven, and written in your Lord's book; ye behoved to cross it: and therefore kiss His wise and unerring providence. Let not the censures of men, who see but the outside of things (and scarce well that), abate your courage and rejoicing in the Lord; howbeit, your faith seeth but the black side of providence, yet it hath a better side, and God shall let you see it.

Learn to believe Christ better than His strokes; Himself and His promises better than His glooms…"For we know that all things work together for good to them that love God," *ergo*, shipwreck, losses, disappointments, ill tongues, loss of friends, houses or country, are God's workmen, set on work, to work out good to you, out of everything that befalleth you.

Let not the Lord's dealings seem harsh, rough or unfatherly, because it is unpleasant. When the Lord's blessed will bloweth cross your desires, it is best in humility to strike sail to Him and to be willing to be laid any way our Lord pleaseth: it is a point of denial of yourself, to be

---

38   Cracked.

as if ye had not a will but had made a free disposition of it to God, and had sold it over to Him; and to make use of His will for your own is both true holiness, and your ease and peace. Ye know not what the Lord is working out of this, but ye shall know it hereafter.

Venture through the thick of all things after Christ, and lose not your Master, Christ, in the throng of this great market.

Let Christ know how heavy, and how many a stone weight you, and your cares, burdens, crosses, and sins are; let Him bear all: make the heritage sure to yourself: get charters and writs passed and through, and put on arms for the battle, and keep you fast by Christ, and then let the wind blow out of what airt[39] it will your soul will not blow in the sea.

I find Christ the most steadable[40] friend and companion in the world to me now: the need and usefulness of Christ is seen best in trials. O, if He be not well worthy of His room! Lodge Him in house and heart.

There is required patience on our part till the summer fruit in heaven be ripe for us: it is in the bud, but there be many things to do before our harvest come. And we take ill with it, and can hardly endure to set our paper face to one of Christ's storms, and to go to heaven with wet feet, and pain, and sorrow.

We love to carry heaven to heaven with us, and would have two summers in one year, and no less than two heavens; but this will not be for us: one, and such an one, may suffice us well enough.

The Man Christ got but one only, and shall we have two?

Be humbled, walk softly; down with your topsail. Stoop, stoop! it is a low entry to go in at heaven's gates.

However matters go, it is our happiness to win new

---

39   Direction.

40   Servicable.

ground daily in Christ's love, and to purchase a new piece of it daily, and to add conquest to conquest, till our Lord Jesus and we be so near other, that Satan shall not draw a straw or a thread betwixt us.

I dare avouch to all that know God, that the saints know not the length and largeness of the sweet earnest, and of the sweet green sheaves before the harvest, that might be had on this side of the water, if we should take more pains: and that we all go to heaven with less earnest and lighter purses of the hoped for sum than otherwise we might do, if we took more pains to win further in upon Christ in this pilgrimage of our absence from Him.

I exhort you in the Lord to go on in your journey to heaven, and to be content of such fare by the way as Christ and His followers have had before you; for they had always the wind on their faces, and our Lord hath not changed the way to us, for our ease, but will have us following our sweet guide.

O, that our souls would fall so at odds with the love of this world as to think of it as a traveller doeth of a drink of water, which is not any part of his treasure, but goeth away with the using: for ten miles' journey maketh that drink to him as nothing! O, that we had as soon done with this world, and could as quickly despatch the love of it.

It cost Christ and all His followers sharp showers and hot sweats ere they won to the top of the mountain. But still our soft nature would have heaven coming to our bedside when we are sleeping, and lying down with us, that we might go to heaven in warm clothes; but all that came there found wet feet by the way, and sharp storms that did take the hide off their face, and found to's and fro's, and up's and down's, and many enemies by the way.

I rejoice that He is come and hath chosen you in the furnace; it was even there where ye and He set tryst;[41] that is an old gate[42] of Christ's. He keepeth the good old fashion with you, that was in Hosea's days (Hosea ii. 14): "Therefore, behold I will allure her, and bring her to the wilderness and speak to her heart." There was no talking to her heart while He and she were in the fair and flourishing city and at ease; but out in the cold, hungry, waste wilderness, He allureth her, He whispered in news into her ear there, and said, "Thou art mine."

When He was in the grave, He came out and brought the keys with Him: He is Lord-jailor: nay, what say I? He is Captain of the castle, and He hath the keys of death and hell: and what are our troubles but little deaths? and He, who commandeth the great castle, commandeth the little also.

There be many Christians, most like unto young sailors, who think the shore and the whole land doth move, when the ship and they themselves are moved; just so, not a few do imagine that God moveth, and saileth, and changeth places, because their giddy Souls are under sail, and subject to alteration, to ebbing and flowing; but the foundation of the Lord abideth sure.

God knoweth that ye are His own. Wrestle, fight, go forward, watch, fear, believe, pray; and then ye have all the infallible symptoms on one of the elect of Christ within you.

Acquaint yourself with Christ's love, and ye shall not miss to find new goldmines and treasures in Christ.

I am just like a man who hath nothing to pay his thousands of debt; all that can be gotten of him, is to seize upon his person. Except Christ would seize upon myself, and make the readiest payment that can be of my heart and love to Himself, I have no other thing to give Him.

---

41 Prearranged meeting.

42 Way, path.

Every man thinketh he is rich enough in grace till he take out his purse and tell his money, and then he findeth his pack but poor and light in the day of a heavy trial. I found I had not to bear my expenses, and should have fainted if want and penury[43] had not chased me to the store-house of all.

Alas, that we should love by measure and weight, and not rather have floods and feasts of Christ's love! O, that Christ would break down the old narrow vessels of these narrow and ebb souls, and make fair, deep, wide, and broad souls, to hold a sea and a full tide, flowing over all its banks of Christ's love.

Ye must take a house beside the Physician: it shall be a miracle if ye must be the first sick man He put away uncured, and worse than He found you. "Him that cometh to Me, I will in no wise cast out." Take ye that; it cannot be presumption to take that as your own, when ye find your wounds stound[44] you;…faith hath sense of sickness, and looketh like a friend to the promise; and looking to Christ therein, is glad to see a known face.

It maketh not much what way we go to heaven; the happy home is all, where the roughness of the way shall be forgotten. He is gone home to a friend's house, and made welcome, and the race is ended.

Look for crosses, and while it is fair weather mend the sails of the ship.

Let Christ's love bear most court in your soul, and that court will bear down the love of other things.

Christ chargeth me to believe His daylight at midnight.

A heart of iron and iron doors will not hold Christ out. I give Him leave to break iron locks and come in, and that is all.

---

43   Extreme want, poverty, destitution.

44   To hurt or cause pain.

I have many a grieved heart daily in my calling. I would be undone, if I had not access to the King's chamber of presence, to show Him all the business.

It were a well-spent journey, to creep hands and feet, through seven deaths and seven hells, to enjoy Him up at the well-head. Only let us not weary: the miles to that land are fewer and shorter than when we first believed; strangers are not wise to quarrel with their host, and complain of their lodging; it is a foul way, but a fair home.

Dear brother, weary not of my sweet Master's chains; we are so much the sibber[45] to Christ that we suffer. Lodge not a hard thought of my royal King. Rejoice in His cross. Your deliverance sleepeth not. He that will come is not slack of His promise. Wait on for God's timeous[46] salvation, ask not when or how long. I hope He shall lose nothing of you in the furnace, but dross.

I rather wish Him my heart than give Him it; except He take it and put Himself in possession of it (for I hope He hath a market-right to me, since He hath ransomed me), I see not how Christ can have me. O, that He would be pleased to be more homely with my soul's love, and to come in to my soul and take His own.

His "well done" is worth a shipful of good-days and earthly honours.

Not one ounce, not one grain-weight more is laid on me than He hath enabled me to bear.…Faith hath cause to take courage from our very afflictions; the devil is but a whetstone to sharpen the faith and patience of the saints. I know He but heweth and polisheth stones for the new Jerusalem.

His cross is the sweetest burden that ever I bare: it is such a burden as wings are to a bird, or sails to a ship, to

---

45 Related to, a sibling of.

46 Timely.

carry me forward to my harbour.

Ye have God's promise, that ye shall have His presence in fire, water, and in seven tribulations.

Come in, come in to Christ, and see what ye want, and find it in Him. He is the short cut (as we use to say) and the nearest way to an outgate[47] of all your burdens. I dare avouch, ye shall be dearly welcome to Him; my soul would be glad to take part of the joy ye should have in Him.

I dare say, angels' pens, angels' tongues; nay, as many worlds of angels as there are drops of water in all the seas, and fountains, and rivers of the earth, cannot paint Him out of you.

Be content to wade through the waters betwixt you and glory with Him, holding His hand fast; for He knoweth all the fords. Howbeit ye may be ducked, yet ye cannot drown, being in His company. Be not afraid, therefore, when ye come even to the black and swelling river of death to put in your foot and wade after Him; the current, how strongsoever, cannot carry you down; the Son of God, His death and resurrection, are stepping stones and a stay to you; set down your feet by faith upon these stones and go through as on dry land; if ye knew what He is preparing for you, ye would be too glad.

I dare not thank myself, but I dare thank God's depth of wise providence, that I have an errand in me, while I live, for Christ to come and visit me, and bring with Him His drugs and His balm.

I but mar His praises; nay, I know no comparison of what Christ is, and what His worth is: all the angels, and all the glorified, praise Him not so much as in halves: who can advance Him or utter all His praises?

I know no sweeter way to heaven, than through free grace and hard trials together, and one of these cannot

---

47   A passage, way out.

well want another.

Christ should be our night song and our morning song.

Blessed be my rich Lord Jesus, who sendeth not away beggars from His house with a toom (empty) dish. He filleth the vessels of such as will come and seek. We might beg ourselves rich (if we were wise), if we could but hold out our withered hands to Christ, and learn to suit and seek, ask and knock.

I am every way in good case, both in soul and body; all honour and glory be to my Lord. I want nothing but a further revelation of the beauty of the unknown Son of God.

I beseech you in the Lord Jesus, beware, beware of unsound work, in the matter of your salvation: ye may not, ye cannot, ye do not want Christ. Then after this day convene all your lovers before your soul; and give them their leave, and strike hands[48] with Christ, that thereafter there may be no happiness to you but Christ; no hunting for anything but Christ; no bed at night (when death cometh) but Christ: Christ, Christ, who but Christ? I know this much of Christ, He is not ill[49] to be found, not lordly of His love; woe had been my part of it for evermore, if Christ had made a dainty of Himself to me; but God be thanked, I gave nothing for Christ; and not I protest, before men and angels, Christ cannot be exchanged; Christ cannot be sold, Christ cannot be weighed.

Because I am His own (God be thanked) He may use me as He pleaseth.

"In all their afflictions He was afflicted." Then Christ bore the first stroke of this cross: it rebounded off Him on upon you, and ye got it at the second hand, and He and ye are halvers in it. And I shall believe for my part, He mindeth to distil heaven out of this loss, and all others

---

48   Clasp hands to seal a deal or agreement between two people.

49   Difficult.

the like; for wisdom devised it, and love laid it on, and Christ owneth it as His own, and putteth your shoulder only beneath a piece of it.

Among many marks that we are on the journey, and under sail towards heaven, this is one, when the love of God so filleth our hearts that we forget to love and care too much for the having or wanting of other things; as one extreme heat burneth out another.

For this cause God's bairns "take well with spoiling of their goods," "knowing in themselves, that they have in heaven a better and an enduring substance." What better and wiser course can ye take than to think that your one foot is here and your other foot in the life to come, and to leave off loving, desiring, or grieving for the wants that shall be made up when your Lord and ye shall meet.

Let our Lord's sweet hand square us and hammer us, and strike off the knots of pride, self-love and world-worship, and infidelity, that He may make us stones and pillars in His Father's house (Rev. iii. 12). Think ye much to follow the Heir of the crown, who had experience of sorrows and was acquainted with grief (Isa. liii. 3).

We see God's decrees when they bring forth their fruits, all actions, good and ill, sweet and sour, in their time; but we see not presently the after birth of God's decree, to wit, His blessed end, and the good that He bringeth out of His holy and spotless counsel. We see His working and we sorrow; the end of His counsel and working lieth hidden and underneath the ground, and therefore we cannot believe.

Even amongst men, we see hewn stones, timber, and a hundred scattered parcels and pieces of a house, all under tools, hammers, and axes, and saws; yet the house, the beauty and ease of so many lodgings and ease-rooms, we neither see nor understand for the present; these are but in the mind and head of the builder as yet. We see red earth, unbroken clods, furrows, and stones; but we see not summer lilies, roses, and the beauty of a garden.

Give Him leave to take His own way of dispensation with you; and though it be rough, forgive Him; He defieth you to have as much patience to Him, as He hath borne to you.…When His people cannot have a providence of silk and roses, they must be content with such an one as He carveth out for them.

Ye would not go to heaven but with company, and ye may perceive that the way of those who went before you was through blood, suffering, and many afflictions; nay, Christ, the Captain, went in over the door-threshold of paradise, bleeding to death.…Christ hath borne the whole complete cross, and his saints bear but bits and chips; as the apostle saith, "the remnants of leavings of the cross."

I find Christ to be Christ, and that He is far, far, even infinite heaven's height above man. And that is all our happiness. Sinners can do nothing but make wounds that Christ may heal them; and make debts, that He may pay them; and make falls, that He may raise them; and make deaths, that He may quicken them; and spin out and dig hells to themselves, that He may ransom them.

Now I will bless the Lord that ever there was such a thing as the free grace of God, and a free ransom given for sold souls; only, alas! guiltiness maketh me ashamed to apply to Christ, and to think it pride in me to put out my unclean and withered hand to such a Saviour!

But it is neither shame nor pride for a drowning man to swim to a rock, nor for a ship-broken soul to run himself ashore upon Christ. Suppose once I be guilty, need force I cannot, I do not, go by Christ.

We take in good part that pride, that beggars beg from the richer. And who is so poor as we? And who is so rich as He who selleth fine gold (Rev. iii. 18)?

Be content, ye are His wheat growing in our Lord's field. And if wheat, ye must go under our Lord's threshing instrument, in His barn-floor, and through His sieve, and through His mill to be bruised, as the Prince of your salvation, Jesus, was (Isa. liii. 10), that ye may be found good bread in your Lord's house.

A king from heaven hath sent for you; by faith He showeth you the new Jerusalem, and taketh you alongst in the Spirit through all the ease-rooms and dwelling-houses in heaven, and saith, "All these are thine, this palace is for thee and Christ"; and if ye only had been the chosen of God, Christ would have built that one house for you and Himself. Now it is for you and many also.

Christ taketh as poor men may give: where there is a mean portion, He is content with less, if there be sincerity; broken sums and little feckless obedience will be pardoned, and hold the foot with Him....He breaketh not a bruised reed, nor quencheth the smoking flax: but if the wind blow, He holdeth His hands about it till it rise to a flame.

I am most gladly content that Christ breaketh all my idols in pieces: it hath put a new edge upon my blunted love to Christ. I see He is jealous of my love, and will have all to Himself.

They are blessed who suffer and sin not, for suffering is the badge that Christ hath put upon His followers: take what way we can to heaven, the way is edged up with crosses....One thing by experience my Lord hath taught me, that the waters betwixt this and heaven may all be ridden, we be well horsed, I mean, if we be in Christ, and not one shall drown by the way.

Now would to God, all cold-blooded,[50] faint-hearted soldiers of Christ would look again to Jesus and to His love; and when they look, I would have them to look again and again, and fill themselves with beholding of Christ's beauty; and I dare say then, that Christ should come in great court and request with many.

Lighten your heart by laying your all upon Him....Frame yourself for Christ, and gloom not upon His cross.

---

50   Cowardly.

I have a lover, Christ, and yet I want love for Him. I have a lovely and desirable Lord, who is love-worthy, and who beggeth my love and heart, and I have nothing to give Him. Dear brother, come further in on Christ, and see a new treasure in Him: come in, and look down, and see angel's wonder, and heaven and earth's wonder of love, sweetness, majesty, and excellency in Him.

Dry wells send us to the fountain.

Christ hath so handsomely fitted for my shoulders this rough tree of the cross, as that it hurteth me no ways. My treasure is up in Christ's coffers; my comforts are greater than ye can believe; my pen shall lie for penury of words to write of them.

No pen, no words, no image can express to you the loveliness of my only, only Lord Jesus.

TO MISTRESS TAYLOR

Mistress,—Grace, mercy, and peace be to you. Though I have no relation worldly, or acquaintance with you, yet (upon the testimony and importunity of your elder son now at London, where I am, but chiefly because I esteem Jesus Christ in you to be in place of all relations) I make bold in Christ to speak my poor thoughts to you concerning your son lately fallen asleep in the Lord (who was sometime under the ministry of the worthy servant of Christ, my fellow-labourer, Mr. Blair, and by whose ministry I hope he reaped no small advantage). I know grace rooteth not out the affections of a mother, but putteth them on His wheel who maketh all things new, that they may be refined; therefore sorrow for a dead child is allowed to you, though by measure and ounce-weights; the redeemed of the Lord have not a dominion or lordship over their sorrow and other affections, to lavish out Christ's goods at their pleasure. "For ye are not your own, but bought with a price"; and your sorrow is not your own, nor hath He redeemed you by halves; and therefore ye are not to make Christ's cross no cross. He commandeth you to weep; and that princely One, who took up to heaven with Him a man's heart to be a compassionate High Priest, became your fellow and companion on earth, by weeping for the dead (John xi. 35). And therefore ye are to love that cross, because it was once on Christ's shoulders before you; so that by His own practice He hath overgilded and covered your cross with the Mediator's lustre. The cup ye drink was at the lip of sweet Jesus, and He drank of it; and so it hath a smell of His breath. And I conceive ye love it not the worse that it is thus sugared; therefore drink, and believe the resurrection of your son's body....I was not a witness to his death, being called out of the kingdom; but ye shall credit those whom I do credit, he died comfortably. It is true, he died before he did so much service to Christ on earth, as I hope and heartily desire your son Mr. Hugh (very dear to me in Christ) shall do. But that were a matter of sorrow, if this were not to counterbalance it, that he hath changed service-houses, but hath not changed services or Master (Rev. xxii. 3). What he could have done in this lower house, he is now upon that same service in the higher house; and it is all one, it is the same service, and the same Master, only there is a change of conditions. And ye are not to think it a bad bargain for your beloved son, where he hath gold for copper and brass, eternity for time. I believe Christ hath taught you (for I give credit to such a witness of you as your son Mr. Hugh) not to sorrow because he died. All the knot[51] must be, he died too soon, he died too young, he died in the morning of his life, this is all; but sovereignty must silence your thoughts. I was in your condition; I had but two children, and both are dead since I came hither. The supreme and absolute Former of all things giveth not an account of any of His matters.

The good husbandman may pluck His roses and gather in His lilies at midsummer, and, for ought I dare say, in the beginning of the first summer month; and He may transplant young trees out of the lower ground to the higher, where they have more of the sun, and a more free air, at any season of the year. What is that to you or me? the goods are His own. The Creator of time and winds did a merciful injury (if I dare borrow the word) to nature in landing the passenger so early.

They love the sea too well who complain of a fair wind and a desirable tide, and a speedy coming ashore, especially a coming ashore in that land where all the inhabitants have everlasting joy upon their heads. He cannot be too early in heaven; his twelve hours were not short hours. And withal, if ye consider this, had ye been at his bed-side, and should have seen Christ coming to

---

51 Problem, difficulty.

him, ye would not, ye could not, have adjourned Christ's free love, who would want him no longer. And dying in another land, where his mother could not close his eyes, is not much. Who closed Moses' eyes? and who put on his winding sheet? For ought I know, neither father, nor mother, nor friend, but God only. And there is as expedite, fair, and easy a way betwixt Scotland and heaven, as if he had died in the very bed he was born in. The whole earth is his Father's; any corner of his Father's house is good enough to die in.

It may be, the living child (I speak not of Mr. Hugh) is more grief to you than the dead. Ye are to wait on, if at any time God shall give him repentance; Christ waited as long possibly on you and me, certainly longer on me....It seemeth that Christ will have this world your step-dame;[52] I love not your condition the worse; it may be a proof that ye are not a child of this lower house, but a stranger. Christ seeth it not good only, but your only good, to be led thus to heaven; and think this a favour, that He hath bestowed upon you free, free grace, that is mercy without hire, ye paid nothing for it. And who can put a price upon anything of royal and princely Jesus Christ? And that God hath given to you to suffer for Him the spoiling of your goods, esteem it as an act of free grace also; ye are no loser, having Himself; and I persuade myself if ye could prize Christ, nothing could be bitter to you. Grace, grace be with you.—Your brother and well-wisher,

S. R.
London, 1645.

---

52   Step-mother.

TO THE LADY EARLSTOUN

Mistress,—Grace, mercy, and peace be to you. I long to hear how your soul prospereth. I exhort you to go on in your journey; your day is short, and your afternoon's sun will soon go down; make an end of your accounts with your Lord; for death and judgment are tides that bide no man. Salvation is supposed to be at the door, and Christianity is thought an easy task, but I find it hard, and the way strait and narrow, were it not but my guide is content to wait on me, and to care for a tired traveller. Hurt not your conscience with any known sin; let your children be as so many flowers borrowed from God; if the flowers die or wither, thank God for a summer's loan of them, and keep good neighbourhood to borrow and lend with Him. Set your heart upon heaven, and trouble not your spirit with this clay idol of the world, which is but vanity, and hath but the lustre of the rainbow in the air, which cometh and goeth with a flying March shower.…My Lord hath been pleased to make many unknown faces laugh upon me, and hath made me well content of a borrowed fireside, and a borrowed bed. I am feasted with the joys of the Holy Ghost, and my royal King beareth my charges honourably.…The great messenger of the covenant, the Son of God, establish you on your rock, and keep you to the day of His coming.—Yours in his sweet Lord Jesus,

Samuel Rutherford.
Aberdeen, March 7, 1637.

For Marion M'Knaught

Loving and dear Sister,—I fear that you be moved and
cast down because of the late wrong that your husband
received in your town-council; but I pray you comfort
yourself in the Lord, for a just cause bides under the water only as long as wicked men hold their hands above it;
their arm will weary, and then the just cause shall swim
above, and the light that is sown for the righteous shall
spring and grow up. If ye were not strangers here, the
dogs of the world would not bark at you (2 Cor. vi. 8).
You shall see all the windings and turnings that are in
your way to heaven out of God's word; for He will not
lead you to the kingdom at the nearest; but you must
go through "honour and dishonour, by evil report and
good report, as deceivers and yet true"; ver. 9, "as unknown and yet well-known, as dying and behold we
live, as chastened and not killed"; ver. 10, "as sorrowful
and yet always rejoicing." The world is one of the enemies that we have to fight with, but a vanquished and
overcome enemy, and like a beaten and forlorn soldier;
for our Jesus hath taken the armour from it: let me then
speak to you in His words. "Be of good courage," saith
the Captain of our salvation, "for I have overcome the
world." You shall neither be free of the scourge of the
tongue, nor of disgraces, even if it were buffetings and
spittings upon the face, as was our Saviour's case, if you
follow Jesus Christ. I beseech you in the bowels of our
Lord Jesus, keep a good conscience (as I trust you do):
you live not upon men's opinions; gold may be gold
and have the king's stamp upon it, when it is trampled
upon by men. Happy are you if, when the world tram-
pleth upon you in your credit and good name, yet you
are the Lord's gold, stamped with the King of heaven's

image, and "sealed by His Spirit unto the day of your redemption." Pray for the Spirit of love (1 Cor. xiii. 7). Love "beareth all things, believeth all things, hopeth all things, endureth all things." And I pray you that your husband, yea I charge you before God and the Lord Jesus Christ, and the elect angels, pray for these your adversaries: read this to your husband from me; and let both of you "put on, as the elect of God, bowels of mercies." And, sister, remember how many thousands of talents of sins your Master hath forgiven you: forgive ye, therefore, your fellow-servants one talent; follow God's command in this, "and seek not after your own heart, and after your own eyes" in this matter, as the Spirit speaks (Num. xv. 39). Ask never the counsel of your own heart here; the world will blow up your heart now, and cause it swell, except the grace of God cause it to fall. Jesus, even Jesus, the eternal Wisdom of the Father, give you wisdom; I trust God shall be glorified in you; and a door shall be opened unto you as the Lord's prisoners of hope, as Zechariah speaks. It is a benefit to you that the wicked are God's fan to purge you; and I hope they shall blow away no corn or spiritual graces, but only your chaff. I pray you, in your pursuit, have so recourse to the law of men that you wander not from the law of God. Be not cast down: if you saw Him, who is standing on the shore, holding out His arms to welcome you to land, you would not only wade through a sea of wrongs, but through hell itself, to be at Him: and I trust in God you see Him sometimes. The Lord Jesus be with your spirit, and all yours.—Your brother in the Lord,

S. R.
Anwoth.

Ye have only these two shallow brooks, sickness and death, to pass through; and ye have also a promise that Christ shall do more than meet you, even that he shall come Himself, and go with you, foot for foot, yea and bear you in His arms. O then! for the joy that is set before you, for the love of the Man (Who is also God over all, blessed for ever) that is upon the shore to welcome you: run your race with patience.

Printed in Great Britain
by Amazon

THE 6 STEPS TO
FINANCIAL
FREEDOM

HOW TO TURN
YOUR DEBT
INTO WEALTH

Vincent Chen

IMMANUEL EZEKIEL

Cover and Interior Design: Adina Cucicov, Flamingo Designs

ISBN: 978-0-9571423-0-5

www.The6StepstoFinancialFreedom.com

Dedicated to my parents Monty and Yvette Ezekiel,
who lived debt-free and happy.

In spite of our modest background,
they taught me the value of money and showed me
the importance of contributing to the community.

Through their love and strong family values,
they inspired me to educate and help other people
to live happier and debt-free lives.

ABOUT THE AUTHOR

AT THE AGE OF sixteen Immanuel Ezekiel left school with only a few basic qualifications and began working on a building site.

Fed up with being poor, he educated himself on how to build wealth by reading books, listening to CDs, and attending seminars.

He used what he learned to create a successful financial management company with more than forty employees and sales of more than £7 million a year. Now he has achieved financial freedom, owning shares in more than 250 properties worth more than £50 million.

Having created a massive passive income for himself, his passion now is helping others escape from debt to achieve their own financial freedom.

Immanuel knows the devastating effect that debt can have on people's health, relationships and lifestyle. He has developed and enhanced a proven formula that gives even people with serious debt problems the right information, mindset, and strategies to transform their lives faster than they could ever imagine.

Through his financial management company and proven techniques, he has helped thousands of people eliminate debt, build wealth, and achieve financial freedom in the fastest time possible.

TABLE OF CONTENTS

List of Wealth Workouts 1

Foreword 3

1. Stepping Off the Debt Treadmill Today 11

   The Worst Possible Outcome 13

   The Pressures of Modern Living 16

   Why Our Education Lets Us Down 17

   How Desire Becomes Debt 19

   The Ostrich Process for Dealing with Debt 20

   Finding the Way Out of Debt Problems 23

   Stopping the Debt Snowball 24

   Destroying Debt and Building Wealth 25

   Achieving Financial Freedom 26

   Moving Beyond Debt 27

2. Starting the Process of Turning Debt Into Wealth 31

   Introducing The Wealth Wheel 32

   Your Perfect Wealth Wheel 38

   The Road to Financial Freedom 39

   The Roadmap to Wealth 42

3. Six Insider Secrets of Becoming Debt-free and Wealthy 45

   To Beat the System You Need to Understand It 46

  Insider Wealth Secret 1: You Can Choose to Be Wealthy 48

   We Are All Potential Millionaires 50

   Choosing the Path to Wealth or Debt 51

   Are You a Wealth Accumulator or a Consumer? 53

   The Future Consequences of the Choices We Make Every Day 58

  Insider Wealth Secret 2: You Don't Need Money to Make Money .. 62

   The Illusion of Money 62

   In The Days When Money Was Real 63

   How Banks Create Money Out of Thin Air 65

Insider Wealth Secret 3: You Can Turn the Wealth Flow Towards You 70
  The Incredible Power of Compound Growth 70
  Turning Compound Growth to Your Advantage 75
  How Banks Can Make 1000% Profit or More on Your Debts 77
  Inflation 80
  The Pension Problem 80
  How Wealth Affects Your Health and Relationships 84
Insider Wealth Secret 4: Debt Can Be Good or Bad 88
  Only Some Assets Build Wealth 91
  Good Debt and Bad Debt 93
  Is Your Own Home An Asset? 94
Insider Wealth Secret 5: There Is a Conspiracy to Make You Spend More 96
  They Need Us to Take Action and Buy 96
  Taking Responsibility 97
  Money is Emotional 98
Insider Wealth Secret 6: Wealthy People Think Differently 107
  1. Commit to Financial Education 107
  2. Challenge Your Beliefs about Money 109
  3. Change Your Wealth Thermostat Setting 110
  4. Connect to Your Own Wealth Personality 112
  5. Choose Advisers Who Know How to Create Wealth 113
4. Six Essential Habits to Eliminate Debt and Become Wealthy Fast 121
  Wealth Habit 1: Set Financial Goals and Measure Current Net Worth 124
    Present Clarity 124
    Future Vision 127
  Wealth Habit 2: Switch Your Spending to Cash Only 131
    Joining the Cash Economy 132
    Dealing with Arrears and Other Problems 134
  Wealth Habit 3: Stop Thinking Monthly and Set a Budget 136
  Wealth Habit 4: Speed Up Debt Repayment 142
    The Debt Destroyer Process 144
  Wealth Habit 5: Spend Your Money More Wisely 160
    Change Your Spending Mindset 161
    The Waste Annihilator Wheel 164
    Money Saving Tips 166

Wealth Habit 6: Start Building for the Future 174
    Establishing an Emergency Fund 174
    The Wealth Building Process 175
5. Six Steps to Creating Wealth and Passive Income from Property ... 185
    The Long-term Potential of Property 186
    The Attractions of UK Property Investment 188
    Comparing Property with Other Investments 189
    How Your Property Grows in Value 190
    Adding the Power of Passive Income 193
    The Property Wealth Wheel 194
Property Profit Secret 1: Psychology of Success 196
Property Profit Secret 2: Profit Immediately 198
Property Profit Secret 3: Positive Cash Flow 202
Property Profit Secret 4: Popular Location 203
Property Profit Secret 5: Pay Creatively 204
Property Profit Secret 6: Plan Your Portfolio 211
    Deciding Your Objectives 212
    Professional Help 214
    Partner with Others 217
6. Six Secrets of Creating Extra Passive Income Streams 221
    Types of Passive Income 223
    Leveraged Income 224
    Creating Your Own Passive Income Stream 226
    The Passive Income Wealth Wheel 227
Passive Income Secret 1: Psychology of Success 228
Passive Income Secret 2: People with Problems 230
Passive Income Secret 3: Product 234
Passive Income Secret 4: Productivity 237
Passive Income Secret 5: Promotion 238
Passive Income Secret 6: Profit 240
Stepping Forward to Financial Freedom 245

LIST OF WEALTH WORKOUTS

THE BOOK CONTAINS THE following "wealth workouts" to help you transform your finances.

1: Your Wealth Wheel
2: Your Wealth Wheel Lessons
3: Consuming Wealth
4: Financial Freedom
5: The Wealth Flow
6: Good or Bad Debt
7: The Consumption Conspiracy
8: Your Wealth Mindset
9: Net Worth
10: Future Goals
11: Cut Up Your Credit Cards
12: Your Budget
13: Your Debt Destroyer Payment
14: Your Debt Destroyer Payment—Order of Priority
15: Waste Annihilator
16: Building for the Future

FOREWORD

I WROTE THIS BOOK because I have seen first-hand how debt ruins peoples' lives and destroys families and relationships in its wake.

I want to show you that, even if you are currently deeply in debt, there is a way to turn things around and start building wealth.

In many years building a successful business advising thousands of others on how to build wealth, I have learned, developed, and enhanced a proven formula that will show you how to:

- Eliminate all of your debt quickly.
- Achieve financial freedom in the fastest possible time.

I know you've probably heard that promise many times before. It usually comes attached to an invitation to sign up for some expensive program or make a commitment to spend your spare time selling obscure products to your family, friends, and to every stranger you meet in the street.

Fear not! Let me assure you that the system and processes I teach in this book do not require you to spend any additional money and can be achieved by using just your existing income.

Simply by following the system and approaches I'll explain here, you can get to a situation where you are:

- Free of debt (however bad your situation now).
- Free from worry about how you will survive in retirement.
- Free to let your children have the future they want.
- Free to stop working ten or fifteen years earlier than you had planned.
- Free to make as much money when you are asleep as you do when you are awake at your day job.

Even if you are deeply in debt right now, you can achieve all of that within a few years from today.

Does all that sound too good to be true?

Well, let me tell you a little about myself and what I do.

- I have built up part-ownership in over 250 properties with a value of more than £50 million.
- I have created a massive passive income for myself and am financially free.
- I have helped thousands of people get out of debt and create their own substantial passive income streams to achieve financial freedom.

I am not telling you this to impress you but to impress upon you what is genuinely and realistically possible in a relatively very short time.

The truth is I'm not some sort of financial genius and I didn't have the advantage of coming from a background where there was a lot of money, wealth, or financial expertise.

Not the Perfect Start

I grew up in what most people would consider a poor family. I am the youngest of four children and always had the hand-me-downs from my older siblings.

My mother worked full time as a dinner lady and my father worked from five o'clock every morning in an abattoir. I was a poor student who was never academically gifted and left school at sixteen with only a couple of basic qualifications to my name.

I then started a four-year apprenticeship as a heating and ventilation engineer. I was earning less than the minimum wage.

I had to wake up every morning at five-thirty to get ready for work. I worked on building sites, using my hands every day. That's what I really call 'work'!

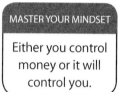

MASTER YOUR MINDSET

Either you control money or it will control you.

As you can imagine, it was not the brightest possible start to my working life and my journey to financial freedom.

I Hated Being Poor

I really wasn't happy with my income and I hated being poor but I always believed there was a different way.

Not that long ago, I was reading books, buying audio tapes and CDs, attending seminars, and listening to speakers talk about how to build wealth and create passive income streams.

I was hungry for knowledge; I wanted to know how to create a better future for myself and my family. I wanted the key to financial freedom and I was prepared to do whatever was needed to learn those secrets.

I now have that knowledge and know those secrets. I want to teach them to you so that you can create a better future for you and your loved ones.

I have learned from some of the greatest financial and personal development minds to emerge in the last twenty years—people like Anthony Robbins, T Harv Eker, Jamie McIntyre, Robert Kiyosaki, Brian Tracy, Zig Ziglar, Napoleon Hill, Bill Bartmann, and Nisandeh Neta—just to name a few of my own coaches.

I have invested heavily—both in time and in money—in my own financial education, and I still continue to do so.

I turned this knowledge into a financial management company and mortgage broker where I had over forty employees and a sales turnover of more than £7 million a year. That is an average of £175,000 of sales income per employee, which is almost six times the industry average.

I then began applying my financial knowledge and personal experience to build up a substantial property portfolio.

Now you may think I had some sort of a financial advantage because I was the owner of a successful business—and that I had a lot of spare cash to invest.

But nothing could be further from the truth. The fact is, I did it primarily with OPM—Other People's Money.

One of my aims in this book is to show you how you can use OPM to become debt-free and achieve financial freedom.

Helping Hundreds of People

The reason I can now comfortably discuss money, peoples' spending habits, and debt, is that through my money management and mortgage brokerage company I have helped thousands of people change their lives by:

- Getting out of debt fast.
- Realising their true earning potential.
- Creating long-term wealth.

I have shown them how to generate massive passive income by using just their own income—and OPM—to become debt-free and achieve financial freedom.

I am now in the very fortunate position of being totally financially free. My large passive income gives me more choices and better choices and it gives me the freedom to choose whether I want to work or never to work again.

> **MASTER YOUR MINDSET**
>
> If you can't handle the money you already have, why would the universe give you more?

It gives me flexibility and greater choices in my life. I can do what I want, when I want, and—most importantly—with whomever I want.

Those are the same choices I want for you, and if you follow my system, the same choices are absolutely possible for you.

It has become my mission to share what I have learned to help others enrich and transform their lives. My goal is to share the knowledge and expertise about money and wealth that I have built up over the last fifteen years.

I am truly frustrated when I see so many people just like you drowning in debt, because I know the real problems and the damaging effects it causes in your stress levels, your health, and your relationships.

And I'm annoyed when I see the truly bad advice that so many people are being given—advice that actually makes their financial situation even worse.

No matter how bad your current debt situation is right now, I will show you that there is a way out. Turning debt into wealth is not only possible, it can be achieved in a much, much shorter timeframe than you imagine.

But only one person can make that transition and transformation in your life and financial wellbeing. That person is YOU, and you have to take action NOW.

The Debt to Wealth Process

I know if you follow what I am teaching in this book, it will make an enormous difference in your life.

- In the book, I will introduce you to a process I created called the **Wealth Wheel.** This is a tool that I have found has helped many people finally take control of their financial lives.
- I will share and explain in detail my **Wealth Wisdom**, which includes a few unbelievable facts and realities that your bank and credit companies don't want you to know.
- And I will provide you with a series of **Wealth Workouts**, which will help you take action starting today. They will help you escape from that terrible treadmill of debt and move instead onto the freeway towards wealth.

As I believe that the way you *think* is crucial to your wealth, I'll also be sharing a few tips on how to **Master Your Mindset** as we work through the chapters.

If you want to know even more and to create even faster wealth, later in this book I will share some information about how you can learn in more detail about these wealth creation systems. In the meantime, if you take to heart what you learn in this book and start implementing these strategies to change your life, financial freedom can be yours in just a few short years.

I am honoured to have you join me on this journey and wish you every success on your amazing transformation from debt to wealth.

Immanuel Ezekiel

1

Stepping Off the Debt Treadmill Today

JOHN AND VICKY STARED at each other across the table as they realised the financial devastation they had created between them.

How could they not have been aware of the depth of debt and financial mess they were in—and this all after fifteen years of happy marriage?

How could two people just on average incomes have racked up £75,000 of debt between them—this debt being on top of their mortgage—without either of them knowing the full picture of the other's debts?

As I slowly sipped my coffee, giving them a few moments to come to terms with the reality of their dire situation, I reflected on just how many other times I'd seen a similar picture during the last few months and years.

> **MASTER YOUR MINDSET**
>
> It's only when you become financially free that you have real choices in your life.

I thought about the story of Mike—a self-employed plumber who had used his personal credit card to cover his business expenses and running costs for those months there wasn't quite enough work or cash coming in.

The problem was that he was using his credit card to finance his personal life as well. As the months went on, the debts just kept on increasing and more and more of his income was disappearing in servicing his interest payments.

He managed from month to month as he was able to use one card to pay off the other but the bills kept increasing—even with the so-called interest-free offers and balance transfers. The truth is these are not free at all as they charge you 3% to 5% upfront, so they actually collect the interest on the first day.

It didn't take too long before, even in the busy months, Mike was barely earning enough to pay his monthly interest charges—never mind his living expenses.

Does this sound like someone you know—maybe intimately? Could it even be you?

Then there was Sue, a young maths teacher who had a great social life and loved to spend her long holidays in exotic locations. Unfortunately she was trying to match the lifestyle of some of her friends who were earning two or three times her salary.

She managed for a while because every other month she'd receive an offer for a new low-interest credit card. Since these companies felt she had a secure job, they were happy to shower her with special offers and credit advances.

She thought as a maths teacher that she was safe with numbers and she became really good at juggling the different balance transfers and interest rates. But there comes a time when the unbelievable deals are proven to be just that—unbelievable.

The Worst Possible Outcome

The problem for John, Vicky, Mike, and Sue—and hundreds of thousands of people just like them—is that their situation is similar to that of a snowball rolling down a hill.

It starts out really small, but the longer it's allowed to continue and gain momentum, the bigger and more dangerous it gets. It will hit the bottom of the hill with a huge crash and cause very serious damage.

In very many years of running a large team of mortgage brokers, I saw these situations too many times—almost daily, in fact. It was too easy to predict how the snowball would crash for each of them:

- For John and Vicky, a breakdown in their relationship and probable divorce. This would not provide any kind of solution to their financial worries; in fact it would make it worse. It's just a common and unhappy outcome of the situation they found themselves in. (Financial problems are the No. 1 reason relationships fail.)

- For Mike, there was big risk that the continued stress and worry about his financial situation—and the effect it was having on his relationship—would lead to serious, perhaps even life-threatening, health problems.

- For Sue, a ruined credit record and possibly even bankruptcy that would—at best—restrict her lifestyle for many years to come and possibly even damage her career.

In my experience, I know that it is almost always possible to stop that snowball running downhill before it grows even bigger and before it does any serious damage.

Depending on the size of the snowball—the debt that has been built up—the task of removing it completely may take a bit of time. But once the debt snowball has been stopped in its tracks, it begins to 'melt' almost immediately. Once it has been stopped, your overall quality of life and your finances immediately change for the better.

Debt is like a snowball rolling downhill. If you let it keep on rolling, it will get out of control and cause serious financial damage. If you take action to stop it now, things start to get better immediately.

I knew there was the prospect of a different outcome for each of them if they were willing to take action now.

- For John and Vicky, a straightforward action plan would see them clear all their debt in eight to twelve years, including their mortgage, by using nothing more than the income they already have.

- For Mike, various steps—including remortgage and negotiations with some of his creditors—would have him back on his feet within a few months and totally debt-free within five to seven years.

- For Sue, a series of small changes would see her clear all her debts within four to five years, without having to get a second job, even if that meant curtailing those exotic trips for a year or two.

STEPPING OFF THE DEBT TREADMILL TODAY

1

The sad reality is that for every one of these situations I've come across, I've seen far too many people make the choice to let the snowball keep on rolling.

While the disastrous outcome of that decision is inevitable, the crisis can be averted.

The Pressures of Modern Living

The truth is that given the way that most people choose to live today, all these experiences are far from unusual. Just a generation ago, life was a lot less complicated than it is now.

People would get a job, save a deposit for a house, buy the furniture they needed, buy a car, go on holiday once a year, and probably pay money into an employer's pension scheme. They would be unlikely to move house very often and probably wouldn't change their jobs many times during their working lives.

They would have had to jump through quite a few hoops to borrow money so they would be unlikely to get too deeply into debt even if they felt they needed some extra cash.

As recently as 1980, the average household debt in the UK was less than half of household income. By 2011, it was 126%.

Part of the increase in debt was due to the rapid rise in property values and decrease in interest rates. This gave people a false sense of security and allowed them to overextend themselves by increasing their borrowing.

The subsequent collapse of property values—and tightening in borrowing criteria—led to problems for many.

Parts of the UK—along with hard-hit areas of the USA—may have fared worse than many other economies in the crisis, but the picture in most developed economies is not significantly different.

In short we are borrowing much more money than ever before to maintain a standard of living and quality of life that has not improved to the same degree.

The problems of John, Vicky, Mike, and Sue may be more extreme than average but they reflect the way most people these days actually run their financial lives.

Why Our Education Lets Us Down
The fact is, nothing you learned at school or from your parents prepared you for managing money in the modern world.

The global financial crisis in recent years shows that even the world's top financial experts let things get out of control. It's not surprising that ordinary people find it difficult too.

The first part of the problem is that in the last twenty-five to thirty years, many more things have been created, invented, or discovered that we want to spend our money on.

Just think about how many of the things you spend money on today didn't even exist in normal day-to-day life a generation ago.

For example:

- Laptop
- iPod
- Sat-Nav in your car
- Mobile phone
- Wide-screen digital TV

Yet these items have all become seen as essentials today.

The second half of the problem is that for businesses to deliver the growth their shareholders demand, they need to invent new products and then sell us whatever they think we can be persuaded to buy. They have to keep creating new things and convincing us we need them. And they have to make us believe that we need them today.

However, they know we have a limited amount of money, so they make it as easy as possible for us to have those products now. The story is always the same:

- *"Get The Latest Version Today"*
- *"Buy Now Pay Later"*
- *"Easy Payment Terms"*
- *"Stay Ahead Of The Curve"*
- *"Start Today"*
- *"Interest Free Credit"*

There is no room for questions such as "Can I afford it?", "Do I need it?" or "Should I wait a bit longer?"

How Desire Becomes Debt

You know what it's like. That new high-density, oversize, internet-ready, flat-screen television that you absolutely must have costs a whopping £1,499. But actually you can have it today and it's only £50 a month for forty-eight months. You can afford that easily.

You don't care at that moment that payments of £50 a month add up to £2,400 over four years. That's £900 more than the cash price! You just want it on your wall this week because one of your neighbours or friends has one already.

That's exactly what the manufacturers, retailers, and credit providers want you to think. And they bombard you daily with advertising messages and special offers until you give in.

It may not be a TV. It may be a car, a suit, a holiday, a home extension, or anything else. The principle is always the same. They want you to think that it's only a few pounds a month so that it becomes an easy decision to buy now.

Most people just think about the monthly payment and this is the single biggest reason why so many people get themselves deep into debt.

It doesn't take long before all the £50 a months combine together and start to eat away at—and finally overwhelm—your monthly income.

If you are spending much more than a quarter (25%) of your net monthly income on debt repayment, you may be storing up problems for the future.

Debt and insolvency advisers tell us that anyone spending more than half their income on debt repayment is at severe risk of serious financial problems or even insolvency.

Yet, all too often, I've seen situations where people are using 50% or even 75% of their income for debt repayment. That doesn't leave much for your normal living costs and day-to-day expenses—let alone putting anything towards building wealth.

Just stop for a moment and think about how much of your monthly income goes on interest and debt repayment.

Is it a comfortable amount or does it leave you with very little to live the lifestyle you want?

In this book, I'm going to show you how to stop letting wealth flow *out* of your life through debt repayments and start keeping it by *building* wealth instead.

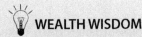 **WEALTH WISDOM**

If you are spending more than half of your income on debt repayments, you are storing up problems for the future—but there is a way to change that quickly.

The Ostrich Process for Dealing with Debt

Recent statistics show that around 10% of all UK households— that's more than 2.5 million families—were at least two months behind on their debt repayments.

That means they are either missing their mortgage payments or unable to pay back the minimum amount on their credit cards or loans.

The approach taken by people in that situation tends to follow a similar pattern. I call this the Ostrich Process because they:

- Get behind on their monthly payments.
- Bury their head in the sand and hope the problem will go away.
- Start to receive demand letters, which they ignore.
- Receive phone calls which start to cause stress.
- Begin to lose sleep and start to suffer problems in their relationship over money.
- Get a major event such as a County Court Judgement.
- Finally decide to do something about it and look for help.

One reason the problem is greater than is generally realised is that most people don't like to talk about money. People who really have money don't shout it from the rooftops while people who have financial problems don't tell anyone either.

> **MASTER YOUR MINDSET**
>
> Financial freedom is the ability to live the lifestyle you want without having to work or rely on anyone else for money.

Those who are in financial straits usually don't know where to go for proper advice and, more often than not, end up getting badly advised—either by people who don't know what they are talking about or by those with vested interests in making even more money from their debt misery.

The sad truth is it's possible to live way beyond your means for quite a long time with the full co-operation—in fact, the active encouragement—of the banks and credit card companies. People like John, Vicky, Mike, and Sue got into difficulties because they had banks and credit card companies lining up to lend them money, and offering great deals to encourage them to take it.

These 'friends' in the credit business that you could rely on to give you cash when you needed it are the very same ones who will happily remove your last penny if you stop making your monthly payments.

The way most people run their finances is not only ruining many lives, it also means a large number of people will reach the end of their working lives still heavily in debt and with no savings to see them through the prospect of many years of retirement.

These are people who could have built significant wealth in their lives but chose to give it away instead to make themselves look and feel good for a brief moment.

If there is only *one* thing you do as a result of reading this book, please make it that you take some sort of action now if you have any debt problems.

Later in this book, I'll explain the actions you should take if you are in that situation.

The solution is probably a lot faster and less painful than you might think. As long as you take action and do something *now*.

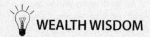

WEALTH WISDOM

Putting your head in the sand and ignoring your debt problems will not make them go away. It simply leaves you with no control and the situation gets worse. Whatever your current situation, there is positive action you can take today.

Finding the Way Out of Debt Problems

The reality for the Johns, Vickies, Mikes, and Sues in the world is that they have made some bad choices that together have created the situation they are in.

They have probably gone through the Ostrich Process and something serious may have happened—a legal letter, a County Court Judgement or repossession—and, by the time they reach that stage, most of them believe it is too late. They cannot see a way out.

They can't imagine how it would be possible to pay off all their debts fast—let alone start building wealth.

For everybody in that situation, financial independence seems like an impossible dream.

I'm not going to pretend that the way out is an easy one but let me reassure you that there is a way out and I'll be explaining it in more detail in this book.

To do is easy. However, *not* to do is easy too!

That debt snowball won't melt overnight but if you take action now and follow the right process and the system that I am going to teach you, it will melt fast.

The first step of the process is stopping the snowball rolling downhill.

Stopping the Debt Snowball

This book is about how you can stop that snowball in its tracks and change your financial situation forever—starting today.

If you are like most people, you probably have significant debts where the payments are eating up large chunks of your monthly income.

Perhaps your debts are limited to the mortgage for your main home and seem quite manageable or perhaps you are burdened with serious problems due to huge debts you have built up on credit cards and other loans.

Either way, you'll find your life will be much better when you get rid of these debts and become totally debt-free as soon as possible.

Even if that situation seems like a dream, you'll discover that making a few small, simple changes and starting to follow the right strategies makes a debt-free life highly achievable in a much shorter timescale than you probably think likely.

Destroying Debt and Building Wealth

In this book, I will introduce you to the Wealth Wheel I created, which gives you a clear picture of how well positioned you are for achieving the financial freedom you desire.

I'll show you how creating a bigger Wealth Wheel will help you reach your desired destination of financial freedom so much faster. We'll look at all of the factors you need to work on to make your journey to financial freedom as smooth and fast as possible.

But first, I'll show you how too much debt is just like a puncture in your Wealth Wheel that not only makes the journey slow and uncomfortable, it could cause you serious problems that might even stop you from reaching your desired destination.

The first part of this book is therefore about how you can make a fast repair to that puncture and get back on the road to financial freedom as soon as possible.

> **MASTER YOUR MINDSET**
>
> Poor people work for their money. The wealthy make money work for them.

My Debt Destroyer system gives you the fastest turnaround strategy and action plan available to turn your current situation quickly from being in debt into one of creating wealth.

When you follow the process I outline, you will have a precise action plan that will help you to get your finances going on the right track from the very first day.

STEPPING OFF THE DEBT TREADMILL TODAY

1

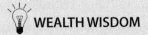

WEALTH WISDOM

The first step towards financial freedom is fixing the punctures that debt causes in your Wealth Wheel so that you can quickly get back on the road to building wealth in your financial life.

Achieving Financial Freedom

You will be able to follow this program wherever you are in your life right now; you don't need to change your job, you don't need to work harder, and you don't need to find additional sources of income.

And it will work even if you are in deep debt right now.

Becoming totally debt-free is easier than you'd believe—you just need someone to show you how.

Most people who have serious debt problems can't even imagine the idea of being free of debt. Yet, for most, it is not only possible, it can be done faster than they ever imagined.

In my experience, even people with serious debt problems have been able to turn their circumstances around and pay off all of their debts—including their mortgage—in five to seven years, or even less. All that can be achieved from income you already have in your life.

This is a change that leads to a better way of life and means you eventually end up enjoying a better lifestyle than you did before—without the stress of debt.

If you have problems with debt, the first aim of this book is to give you a viable escape route with a clear destination.

Moving Beyond Debt

But I want to go beyond getting you out of debt. I want to give you the tools and strategies you need to take a completely new approach to your finances.

So, as well as giving you the escape route from debt, I'm going to show you how you can build your wealth even further.

I'm going to show you how to build your Wealth Wheel to put you in a much better situation financially than you are now. I'll show you how anyone can become financially free using carefully planned wealth-building strategies.

While everything we talk about up to this stage can be done with your existing job and income, you can get completely different results if you are willing to look at ways to add new sources of income.

That may be something alongside your existing job or it may be something you see as replacing your current job.

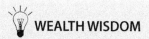
WEALTH WISDOM

Creating the best possible Wealth Wheel can deliver you passive income that gives you the financial freedom of being able to choose when you work and what you do.

Later in this book, I'll show you how you can build a Wealth Wheel that gives you the kind of financial future that most others can only dream about.

Even if you have maxed out on your credit options, this process can enable you to be debt-free in as few as five to seven years.

When you've followed that process, your situation will be transformed and you will be ready to build serious wealth in the future.

Today you can begin the journey from debt to wealth. You could move from a situation of having to work for money to having your money work for *you*—using money you already bring home.

Just imagine what your life would be like if you had no debts. Just imagine a life where you could do what you wanted—and pay for it in cash.

It really is possible—so let's get started.

💡 WEALTH WISDOM SUMMARY:
Section 1

- Debt is like a snowball rolling downhill. If you let it keep on rolling, it will get out of control and cause serious financial damage. If you take action to stop it now, things start to get better immediately.

- If you are spending more than half of your income on debt repayments, you are storing up problems for the future—but there is a way to change that quickly.

- Putting your head in the sand and ignoring your debt problems will not make them go away. It simply leaves you with no control and the situation gets worse. Whatever your current situation, there is positive action you can take today.

- The first step towards financial freedom is fixing the punctures that debt causes in your Wealth Wheel so that you can quickly get back on the road to building wealth in your financial life.

- Creating the best possible Wealth Wheel can deliver you passive income that gives you the financial freedom of being able to choose when you work and what you do.

2

Starting the Process of Turning Debt Into Wealth

STARTING ON THE JOURNEY from debt to wealth is rather like any other journey you might make in your life.

You need to know where you are now, where you are going, and how you are going to get from one point to the other.

The Wealth Wheel is a concept I created that has helped many people with all of these steps.

It acts as an overall snapshot of your financial life based on where you think you currently are. It also helps you define where you want to go and allows you to work out the steps you'll need to take to get there.

First, I'll introduce you to the key elements—or spokes—of the wheel and then show you how to use it to help with your journey.

Introducing The Wealth Wheel

The six spokes of the wheel are as follows:

1. **Debt:** Outstanding loans, mortgages, credit card balances or any other money you owe.
2. **Work Income:** Income you earn from your normal job.
3. **Emergency Savings:** Easily-accessible money you have put aside for a "rainy day."
4. **Retirement Fund:** Income or savings you will draw on when you finish work.
5. **Property:** Your main home and holiday home if you want one.
6. **Passive Income:** Income you earn without having to do any additional work e.g. royalties, rent or investment income.

The Wealth Wheel

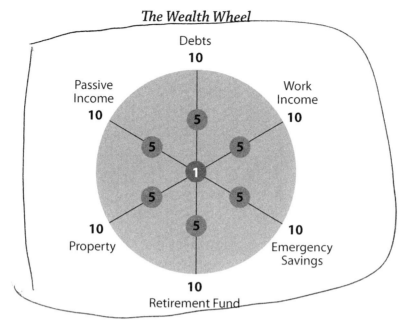

Using a scale of 1 to 10, the Wealth Wheel works using your assessment of your current situation for each element of the wheel. This will demonstrate how well equipped you currently are for the road to wealth. Your ratings will show how smooth a journey you are having and what your progress is likely to be if you continue on the same path.

To use the Wealth Wheel, look at each spoke of the wheel and rate yourself according to how you feel about your current situation in relation to that element. The scale for the ratings is as follows:

10 (the outside edge of the wheel) is the best possible situation you could be in or where you want to be.

5 (the mid-point of the wheel) is the halfway house—you are not quite there but well on your way.

1 (the centre of the wheel) is the rating you would give if you are nowhere near or haven't even started.

You can choose a rating anywhere between 1 and 10 but I have provided definitions for 1, 5 and 10 as a guide. I'll now explain in a bit more detail what each of these ratings means.

1. Debts

This covers any debts such as loans, credit cards, home improvement loans, store cards, hire purchase agreements, and mortgages.

10 is debt free.

5 is if you are spending less than 50% of your net income on debt repayment (including your mortgage).

1 is where your monthly outgoings exceed your regular monthly income.

2. Work Income

This reflects whether your current work income allows you to live the lifestyle you desire—for example, whether it enables you to live in the house you want, eat in the restaurants you like, go on holiday where and when you choose and drive the car you want.

10 is where you only spend 80% of what you earn and you can afford whatever you want from your work income.

5 is where you can afford most things but you still check the menu and choose based on the price. You spend almost all of your earnings each month.

1 is where your money usually runs out before the end of the month and you can't afford to buy any of the things you really want.

3. Emergency Savings

This is your buffer zone to help you in emergencies, to cover you in times of ill-health or unexpected bills.

10 is where you have easily-accessible savings that would cover your normal monthly living expenses for six to twelve months.

5 is where you could cover your normal monthly living expenses for three to six months.

1 is where you have no savings whatsoever.

4. Property

Are you living in your ideal house, and if you want a holiday home, do you have that too?

10 is where you are living in your ideal home and also have a holiday home (if you want one).

5 is where you are getting there.

1 is where you haven't even started on the property ladder yet.

5. Retirement Fund

This is about the retirement fund you have built up that will give you a regular income whenever you choose to retire.

10 is where you **already have** a retirement fund that will produce the same income as you are on now. So, if you earn £30,000 a year, at a return of 5% you will need twenty times that sum (£600,000) to provide an annual income of £30,000.

5 is where you have a fund that will give you 50% of your total annual income.

1 is where you have made no provision whatsoever.

6. Passive Income

This is where you make an investment or do a job once and then get paid for it over and over again without having to do any more work trading your time for money.

Examples could be royalties on a book you have written or rental income on a property you own.

10 is where your passive income is **already** greater than all your monthly expenses, including food, loan costs, etc.

5 is where you have 50% of your normal monthly expenses covered by passive income and you are continuing to build it.

1 is where you have no passive income at all.

While the whole picture of your finances is a little more complicated, the Wealth Wheel reflects the main areas most people need to cover to become financially free and wealthy.

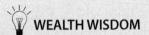

WEALTH WISDOM

When your Wealth Wheel is off-balance, your journey to financial freedom will be long and uncomfortable and reaching your desired destination will be challenging.

Now that you know how the Wealth Wheel works, I recommend that you take a few minutes to complete your own Wealth Wheel based on your current assessment of your situation.

WEALTH WORKOUT 1: YOUR WEALTH WHEEL

Complete your own Wealth Wheel by giving each spoke a score of 1 to 10 based on the above ratings.

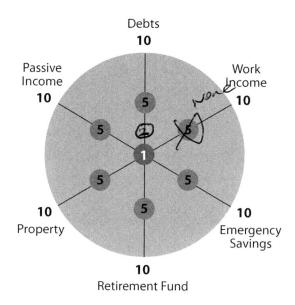

So how does your Wealth Wheel look?

It is a nice round wheel of perfect 10s?

Or is it a mixed picture that presents challenges?

If your wheel is very uneven—or if many of your numbers are much lower than 10—don't worry. The rest of this book is about fixing your Wealth Wheel and making it as big as possible.

This will help you cover more ground faster and have an easier route to financial freedom!

WEALTH WORKOUT 2: YOUR WEALTH WHEEL LESSONS

Now write out some notes about what you have learned from your own Wealth Wheel.

What's good about it, what isn't, which areas do you need to work on?

Your Perfect Wealth Wheel

Many people find the Wealth Wheel useful because it gives them a clear way to measure to important points in their journey to financial freedom. It clarifies where you are now and where you want to go.

The exercise you have just completed has given you a clear picture of where you are now.

It also helps you define your desired destination because your perfect Wealth Wheel shows you what financial freedom looks like. On the basis of the wheel, financial freedom is when you score as close to perfect 10s as possible.

This is what it would mean for each of the six criteria:

1. **Debts**: Debt free.
2. **Work Income**: You only spend 80% of what you earn and you can afford whatever you want from your main source of income.
3. **Emergency Savings**: You have easily-accessible savings that would cover your normal monthly living expenses for six to twelve months.

4. **Property:** You are living in your ideal home and also have a holiday home (if you want one).
5. **Retirement Fund:** You have built up a fund for retirement that will produce the same income as you are on now.
6. **Passive Income:** Your passive income is already greater than all your monthly living expenses.

In short, financial freedom is the ability to do what you want in your life without having to work for it and without having to think about money.

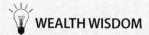 **WEALTH WISDOM**

When your Wealth Wheel is in perfect balance, you have achieved financial freedom and can choose how you spend your time.

The Road to Financial Freedom

Let's now look at the steps you need to take to have the best possible Wealth Wheel.

In psychology, the Kübler-Ross model is widely used to describe how people react to dealing with a life-changing or life-threatening event.

It was originally developed in response to studies of how people deal with news that they are dying, but is now more commonly used to explain how people handle grief or other major traumatic events such as divorce or loss of job.

2

2

STARTING THE PROCESS OF TURNING DEBT INTO WEALTH

The five stages of grief that people are said to go through are:

1. **Denial:** "This can't be happening to me."
2. **Anger:** "Why me? It's not fair."
3. **Bargaining:** "If I could just have a little more time."
4. **Depression:** "What's the point in doing anything about it?"
5. **Acceptance:** "I can't change the situation so I may as well live with it."

As with all similar models, it does not apply to everyone. Not everyone goes through all of these stages and not necessarily in that order. However, I have found that people facing up to the problem of serious debt often go through similar stages.

The problem with this process is that while dealing with grief or terminal illness, you have to accept the situation. But when you're in debt, acceptance is *never* the appropriate end point for the process.

In dealing with debt, acceptance is the *beginning* of the process, not the end.

However, I have identified a six-step process that you need to go through in order to turn debt into wealth:

1. **Awareness** of the problem.
2. **Acceptance** of need to change.
3. **Assessment** of your current financial situation.
4. **Action** to change your situation.
5. **Acceleration** of debt repayment to financial freedom.
6. **Accumulation** of real wealth.

Following these six steps can take anyone from a situation of facing serious debt into one where they are not only out of debt but also enjoying significant wealth.

1. **Awareness of the problem:** Before you can turn the situation around, you have to understand how people get into debt and why it's essential—and possible—to change the situation. I'm going to share some facts about money that demonstrate how banks, credit card companies, retailers and manufacturers manipulate your behaviour by holding back the truth in their advertising.

2. **Acceptance of need to change:** When you've understood the severity of the situation, you need to be willing to make changes in the way you live your life. That means you will have to develop a different approach to spending your money. But it doesn't have to mean a life of austerity. I'll show you some changes you need to make in the way you think and behave about money which will ensure you start seeing fast results.

3. **Assessment of your current financial situation:** The next step in the process is sitting down and working out the exact numbers to get a clear assessment of where you are and working out what you need to do next. I'll give you a series of steps that will enable you to do that.

4. **Action to change your situation:** When you know what you need to do, it's time to take action. I'll give you all the tools you need to create your own specific action plan to turn your debt into wealth using the money you already have.

5. **Acceleration of debt repayment to financial freedom:** Your top priority needs to be getting out of debt so I'll show you exactly what you need to do to turn the situation around. You'll be amazed at how fast you see results by making a few simple changes. You'll get a step-by-step system for doing this as quickly as possible.

6. **Accumulation of real wealth:** The final step in the process is the best of all as it allows you to turn your situation from one of being in debt into starting to build a fund that will provide financial freedom for your future. The processes and mind-set you learn will prepare you to do this faster than you ever thought possible.

The Roadmap to Wealth

The rest of this book takes you through these stages so that you can build the biggest Wealth Wheel you want.

- In chapter 3, I cover six Insider Secrets of Wealth that will help make you **Aware** of why debt is such a big problem and how to escape from it before it's too late.

- In chapter 4, I share six essential habits that help you **Accept** the need for change. I'll show you how to **Assess** where you currently stand and take **Action** to change the situation.

- Chapter 4 also helps you begin the process of escaping from debt by **Accelerating** debt repayment and starting to move towards financial freedom.

- In chapters 5 and 6, I'll share various strategies that help you start to **Accumulate** real wealth and build a strong source of passive income.

The deeper the debt, the longer it will generally take to escape. But it also depends on the strength of your desire for a different way of life and how ready you are to make changes to the way you live.

I've found that most people can see significant changes in their financial situation in a matter of months. Even those who start out deeply in debt can have it all repaid (including their mortgage) in around five to seven years or even less. After that, the only question is how much wealth you want to build.

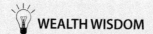 **WEALTH WISDOM**

Following the right map, you can escape from debt and reach financial freedom faster than you might think.

2

STARTING THE PROCESS OF TURNING DEBT INTO WEALTH

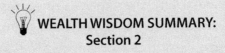

WEALTH WISDOM SUMMARY:
Section 2

- When your Wealth Wheel is off-balance, your journey to financial freedom will be long and uncomfortable and you may never reach your desired destination. You need to take immediate action to improve your Wealth Wheel balance.

- When your Wealth Wheel is in perfect balance, you have achieved financial freedom and can choose how you spend your time.

- Following the right map, you can escape from debt and reach financial freedom faster than you probably think.

3

Six Insider Secrets of Becoming Debt-free and Wealthy

IT'S REMARKABLE THAT, IN the modern world, there is virtually no serious financial education taking place—whether in the school, the workplace, or in business.

From the person working behind the counter at your local bank to some of the most senior legislators and regulators, even people who deal with money every day have very little idea how it works.

In any system, you leave yourself very exposed if you don't understand what is going on.

You are therefore at a huge disadvantage if you don't know the truth about money.

So, before you start taking the necessary action to get out of debt, it's important to know a bit more about how money and wealth creation works.

To Beat the System You Need to Understand It

In this section, I'm going to share some of the insider secrets I've learned about money and wealth.

I have discovered this information through years of study as well as through my own experience running a business of mortgage and wealth advisers and building my own sources of passive income.

Some of the facts I share here are things that others—such as your bank or credit card company or the manufacturers and brands that want you to spend money with them—would rather you didn't know.

But I'm pretty sure that you, like many of the others I've shared this information with, will clearly see how much it is costing you *not* to know these facts.

I'm certain that, when you have this knowledge, you'll be ready to make some changes in your life right away and that you will be much the better for it.

All my experience of wealth has brought home to me the fact that your wealth increases in proportion to your knowledge about it. So I'd strongly recommend that you invest time and money in courses, books and audio programs to help you build your expertise about wealth.

Here are the six insider secrets we'll be looking at:

1. You can choose whether or not to be wealthy.
2. You don't need money to make money.
3. You can turn the wealth flow towards you.
4. You can have good debt and bad debt.
5. You are facing a conspiracy of consumption.
6. You have to think differently to be wealthy.

3

SIX INSIDER SECRETS OF BECOMING DEBT-FREE AND WEALTHY

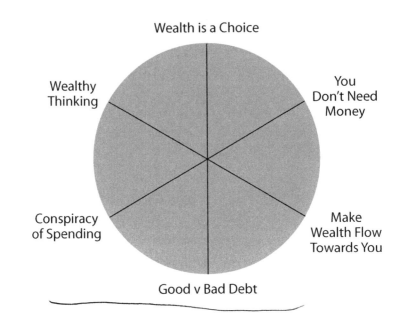

INSIDER WEALTH SECRET 1:
YOU CAN CHOOSE TO BE WEALTHY

It may seem a bit odd to suggest that being wealthy is a matter of choice.

After all, depending on your beliefs, you may think wealth is a matter of hard work or luck or being willing to take risks.

Of course it depends on how you define wealth—whether you measure it in terms of expensive possessions or in terms of financial security.

For example, do you think that someone who lives in a large, smart house and drives an expensive car can be considered as wealthy?

During the depths of the recent financial crisis, I knew many people who had very expensive cars parked permanently outside their homes because they couldn't afford to fill them with petrol.

They were also behind on their mortgage payments and often at risk of repossession or enforced sale of their homes.

Would you still consider them to be wealthy?

What would you say about someone living in a more modest house and driving a second-hand car? Would you consider them to be wealthy?

> **MASTER YOUR MINDSET**
>
> Most people don't get what they want in life because they don't know what they want.

Would you think differently if you knew they had built substantial savings and were about to retire early and travel around the world, looking forward to a secure income for the rest of their lives?

Now, I'm not going to come out with one of these lines that suggest money doesn't matter as long as you are happy. The brutal reality is that people who say money doesn't matter are usually BROKE.

They are trying to kid themselves that they don't really need money but that's often a cover for serious financial problems.

The only time money doesn't matter is when it is no longer an issue in your life. That only happens when you know you have enough money to do whatever you want to do.

However, wealth is not measured by your lifestyle or by the car you drive, the house you live in or where you go on holiday.

True wealth is when you achieve FINANCIAL FREEDOM.

Financial freedom will therefore mean different things to different people. For some, it will be the ability to travel the world staying in the best hotels and not looking at the prices when they make a booking.

For others, it is simply living somewhere they are happy, knowing that all the bills will be paid whether or not they choose to go out to work.

We Are All Potential Millionaires

The ideal position to be in is to have built up enough wealth in your life to allow you to choose what to do—where to live, whether to work, and how to spend your time.

That may seem like an idea that is beyond the reach of most average people.

But consider this:
- The average UK income is currently around £30,000 a year.
- The average working lifespan is around forty years.

Simple multiplication says that, on today's numbers, the average person will earn more than £1,200,000 over their working life.

Yet the harsh reality is that only a handful of people achieve financial freedom during their lives. Where does that £1,200,000 go to?

Well of course a large chunk of it goes in tax and in essential expenses such as buying your home and paying the daily bills.

But the key point is that we have that money in our lives and most of us choose to let it go.

Most people finish their working lives wondering how they are going to survive in retirement. They may be facing downsizing their home and cutting their standard of living because they have not held on to their wealth—never mind made it grow.

Somehow they have let more than £1 million slip through their fingers and they are left with very little.

Choosing the Path to Wealth or Debt

Our financial situation in our middle and later years is a direct consequence of the decisions we make and the habits we develop early on.

- In our twenties, we begin the habits that tend to follow us for the rest of our lives. We start earning money and we either decide to spend it as fast as it comes in or we tailor our spending to put a little aside for the future. We are often tempted not to worry too much about the future as we know we'll be earning more soon.

- In our thirties, we start to take on more responsibilities and there is always the pressure to live in a bigger house, drive a smarter car, and give the kids some of the things we never had ourselves. We choose whether to give in to that pressure or whether to take a longer term view.

- By our forties, responsibilities are increasing along with the pressure of showing an even better standard of living. The choices we have made in the past are already catching up with us. Often the increased income we expected has never really materialised or at least has never kept pace with the demands for increased expenditure.

- In our fifties, we can either be winding down with all our major debts repaid or our dreams have gone and we are worried about how we are going to survive in retirement. We could even be scared that we won't hang on to our jobs until then.

Two people who started out in similar situations and earned the same money during their lives can end up in entirely different situations.

Depending on the choices you make in your life, it is quite possible to reach your fifties—or even earlier—with all your debts repaid and enough passive income to allow you to stop working early and still enjoy a great lifestyle.

Alternatively, at that stage, you could be looking ahead to twenty more years of work with a limited standard of living.

The truth is it is never too late to give up the bad habits you picked up early on and to correct your mistakes.

Whatever your current situation, I want to reassure you that there is a way to make it better quickly.

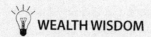

WEALTH WISDOM

The average person in the UK will earn more than £1,200,000 over their working life but most let it slip through their fingers.

Are You a Wealth Accumulator or a Consumer?

The choices you make about what to do with the money you make during most of your life will determine the financial situation you end up in later.

With every penny that comes in to your life, you have to make a choice. You can let that money flow out of your life by giving it to others through:

- Buying goods you don't need.
- Paying too much in tax.
- Wasting a fortune in interest and bank charges.

Alternatively, you can take control of your own wealth and keep it in your own life to give yourself the best future possible.

The outcome for you will depend on which of the following categories best describes you:

- **Wealth accumulator:** You live as if you earn half of what you really do. You will end up rich and will be able to enjoy virtually anything you want in the future.

- **Consumer:** You behave as if you earn twice as much as you really do but you will end up poor and working in your retirement years.

Let's look at the difference between those two categories through the examples of two different couples.

Pete and Jo

After Pete and Jo got together in their twenties, they wanted a really smart house so they sought the biggest mortgage they could get and moved in right away.

That set the pace for the next few years as they kept on moving and making their mortgage bigger.

They live a great lifestyle in a smart £400,000 house, have two luxury cars, send their kids to a great school, and go on two foreign holidays every year.

However, over the years, as their lifestyle has grown, so have their debts. They have increased their mortgage to cover school fees and used credit cards and loans to finance other purchases.

Pete is too worried about the security of his job to even think about the fact that retirement is not far away and they have virtually no savings put aside.

The reality they face at the moment is that they are still stuck with the mortgage for several more years and they have plenty other debts to pay before they even consider saving for retirement.

At least they are in fairly good health—for now—so they should be able to continue working for a few more years—provided they still have jobs.

Despite their lifestyle of smart house, two cars and exotic holidays, Pete and Jo have a lot of debt and they have no significant wealth.

The truth is they have been living a lifestyle they can't afford. They have been renting a dream based on expectation of future income and now they have been handed the bill.

Paul and Jan

Meanwhile, their old college friends Paul and Jan have followed the same career path. You wouldn't guess it to look at their lifestyles but they have earned similar money over the years and their families are around the same age.

Paul and Jan live in a comfortable, smaller home, drive a reliable second-hand car, their kids go to a state school and they only take occasional holidays.

> MASTER YOUR MINDSET
>
> Wealth flows to the accumulator. Wealth flows away from the consumer.

They have lived in a different way from their friends ever since their twenties, when they decided to rent a flat for a year or two. They wanted to save up some cash and acquire furniture and other household items before buying their own home.

When they bought their own home, they chose something that suited their long-term needs and they planned on staying there for a while.

They have been careful to save up for important purchases and they have bought carefully at the sales, in special offers and even second-hand. Though they are not really into do-it-yourself, they manage to do a few odd jobs around the home and paint it themselves.

They have planned their holidays carefully, going to the same cottage most years but they have enjoyed a couple of more exotic trips on special occasions.

It may sound like a relatively frugal lifestyle but they have lived comfortably and happily having most of what they really wanted. They have simply planned well and avoided waste.

Now in their forties, they are looking forward to the kids leaving school and going off to college. They are happy in their home and feel no need to move.

They've got some cash set aside to help the kids through college but they encourage them to get part-time jobs too so that they get used to handling money.

Paul and Jan will pay off their mortgage this year and they have no other debts. They already have built up some passive income for the future and will continue to focus on that over the next few years.

With all their responsibilities taken care of, they are talking about early retirement. But first they are going to take that special long holiday they've always dreamed about.

**Because of the choices they have made, Paul and Jan
have a comfortable lifestyle, they have virtually no debt,
and they are building significant wealth for the future.**

The two couples have not earned significantly different amounts during their life and have not had different needs over the years.

They have simply chosen to spend their money differently.

If you are reading this book, you may well feel that your life looks more like the first couple.

Maybe you feel that most of every penny you earn goes straight out the door to pay your creditors rather than flowing into your own coffers to give you a better future.

Looking back, you may wish you had done some things a little differently over the years. Do you think it's too late to change?

Are you going to have to live with the consequences?

The bad news is that you *do* have to face the consequences.

But the good news is that you *don't* need to live with them long-term. You can deal with them *now*.

What you will learn in the rest of this book will show you how to make different choices from now on so that you can start to turn your debt into wealth. It is never too late to change.

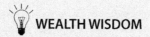 **WEALTH WISDOM**

"Wealth accumulators" live as if they earn half of what they really do but they end up rich and can enjoy anything they like. "Consumers" behave as if they earn twice as much but they end up poor and working in their retirement years.

The Future Consequences of the Choices We Make Every Day

There's a story that the legendary investor Warren Buffett refused to buy a new car because he hated thinking about the millions it would cost him!

If that sounds crazy, consider this...

An average monthly car payment of £350 invested over forty years at 8% a year would produce a fund of more than £1.1 million.

That's why wealthy people like Warren Buffett think about the FUTURE VALUE of every penny they spend—not simply today's cost.

Every penny you spend each day has a long-term cost that is huge compared to the impact it makes in your wallet or in your pocket that day.

When you think of something costing only a few pennies or "just a few quid," these small amounts soon pile up and can build to an astonishing amount over a few years.

When you stop at Starbucks or your local coffee shop on the way into work and pick up that cappuccino, you don't even think about the cost.

Well consider this. If you spend just £2 on that cup of coffee each working day for thirty-five years, what do you think it costs? £10 a week for thirty-five years makes about £18,200. It sounds a lot when you put it like that.

But the truth is even worse. What would have happened if you had invested that money instead?

At 8% interest, £10 a week invested for thirty-five years would have given you a shocking £88,000. That's a pretty expensive cup of coffee—especially when you think about the times you never even finished the cup!

But how many more small expenditures like that are killing your wealth?

Eating out is another great example. Many people blow a fortune on this. Say you spend £90 a week on eating out over thirty-five years, which has cost you a staggering £750,000 in lost investment potential (assuming 8% a year interest).

And how about that £5 a day you spend at the sandwich shop—instead of making your own at home—that's costing you £220,000 over 35 years of your working life.

Maybe you think that 8% a year looks a bit unrealistic in today's financial environment. However, later in this book, I'll be showing you how that sort of return is very achievable over the long term for the educated investor.

So let's just add up the cost over thirty years of grabbing a coffee on your way to work, buying lunch in the sandwich shop and eating out a few times a month.
- Daily takeaway coffee at £2 a day = £88,000 over 35 years.
- Daily sandwiches at £5 a day = £220,000 over 35 years.
- Regular eating out at £90 a week = £750,000 over 35 years.

All three of these together effectively present you with a bill of over £1 million in a few years' time.

Are you beginning to get an idea where your missing millions have gone? Can you see how these small lifestyle choices you are making now are costing you so much in the future?

And here's what makes these numbers even worse. If you are spending money on these items when you are also paying interest on debts, the real cost to you is even higher as you have to take the debt interest—usually at much higher rates—into account.

That £50 meal out is delaying your debt repayment and may be costing you 20% interest or even more.

When you are facing poverty in retirement, do you think you'll feel it was money well spent? And that's all just for starters.

When you start to take into account the money you spend on holidays, clothes, entertainment, and everything else, you'll realise that you are choosing NOT to be a millionaire because of the small luxuries you allow yourself now.

Of course, I'm not going to say that life should be without pleasures. However I do say that you have to make these choices taking into account what you are giving up.

It is not about living a frugal life. It is about planning and making the right choices.

So every penny you spend is not just about loss of money—it's the loss of what you could have earned from it instead.

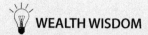

WEALTH WISDOM

The real cost of something you buy is not what you pay for it but what you give up in the future by having spent that money rather than invested it.

WEALTH WORKOUT 3: CONSUMING WEALTH

Answer the following questions to determine whether you are a wealth accumulator or a consumer. Rate each on scale of 1 to 10 depending on how much you agree with it, where 10 is strongly agree and 1 is strongly disagree.

	Rating 1—10
I buy ready meals rather than buying ingredients and cooking myself.	
I usually buy goods without negotiating a special price or better deal.	
I pay off less than the total due on my credit card every month.	
I tend to replace clothes and household goods before they need it.	
I have more than one of most leisure goods such as TVs, computers, music players, etc.	
I save very little each month.	
I have bought many things I never used and regret buying.	
I usually use my credit card or other way of borrowing money such as lease or payment terms for major purchases.	

The higher your score the more you are a Consumer. The lower your score the more you are a Wealth Accumulator.

INSIDER WEALTH SECRET 2:
YOU DON'T NEED MONEY TO MAKE MONEY

One of the biggest myths about wealth is the idea that you need money to make money.

For a long time, like many other people, I believed that the only way to build wealth was either by having substantial funds of your own to invest or by going cap in hand to borrow money from a bank or other financial institution.

This belief was based on the idea that banks already have money to lend you. What a misconception that turned out to be!

What I'm about to share with you will probably shock you in the same way that it has shocked so many others. Although the recent financial crisis has undermined peoples' confidence in banks, most people probably still believe that at the very least, *money is real*.

The Illusion of Money

People go to banks and financial institutions because they think these institutions have money. In fact, the truth is quite shocking.

Money, in the sense that most people think of it, is pretty much an illusion. But it's an illusion that works entirely in the favour of these big institutions—with the support of governments.

The way modern economies are set up, governments and businesses depend on this system being perpetuated. The system is fed by debt and depends on debt to survive.

The biggest victims of this system are the people like you who borrow money from these institutions. People borrowing money are needed to make the system work but they are the ones who then suffer from it in so many ways.

For those people—just like John, Vicky, Mike, and Sue in the introduction—debt can wreck their lives if they take the wrong steps.

To understand the implications of all this in today's world, we need to take a step back in the story of money. Way back in the early days, life was all about simple survival and people did their own hunting, home building and gathering food.

As life gradually became more sophisticated—and communities became larger—people began to develop specialist skills and acquire more possessions. They therefore needed a way to trade skills and goods.

> **MASTER YOUR MINDSET**
>
> The most dangerous words you ever say are "I know that." It shuts off your mind and doesn't allow you to learn.

If I have a sheep and you have a cow, we can do a trade as long as you want a sheep and I want a cow. But this system obviously has its limits and it was clear some form of recognised universal 'currency' was needed.

In The Days When Money Was Real

At first, virtually anything that people could see as having a secure value would be traded—anything from shells to grains of corn to beans or jewellery.

These too had their limits as trading grew in importance and people's needs developed. So, over time, precious metals such as gold and silver became seen as having a clear value—whether as bars, jewellery, or coins.

All of these have one thing in common and that is that they have intrinsic value. In other words, they exist and you can do something with them. This is known as "commodity money."

When valuables such as gold and silver began to be used, people didn't want to keep these in their own homes. So they would leave their silver and gold in the possession of a local merchant, goldsmith or silversmith, who would give them a piece of paper confirming that they had deposited the gold or silver with him.

The problem with this system was that people didn't really want to go back to the merchant and draw out their gold and silver every time they wanted to make a trade. So they started to hand over the pieces of paper when trading with others instead.

These paper notes were the beginning of what is known as "representative money," where the piece of paper is used to represent a real asset that you own.

These merchants and goldsmiths noticed that people never actually came in to withdraw their silver and gold, so they began to lend these assets out to others in exchange for a payment of interest.

When the people who actually owned the assets found out this was happening, they demanded a share of this interest in exchange for leaving their assets on deposit.

On more than one occasion, a problem arose: the total amount of silver and gold the merchants were lending was greater than the amount they held on deposit. This meant that if everybody demanded their gold back at once, there would not be enough to repay everyone.

When people realized this was happening, they were outraged. But, by then, it was too late. Whole economies had become dependent on the availability of these loans and neither governments nor merchants really wanted to abolish the system. So governments stepped in to regulate it instead.

How Banks Create Money Out of Thin Air

This was the beginning of the Fractional Reserve System that is the basis of how the banking system works today. What this means is that it is perfectly legal for banks to lend money they don't have as long as they work within specified limits.

When the Bank of England initiated this system in 1694, the ratio allowed was 2:1. In other words, if a bank held £1,000 in deposits, it could lend £2,000 on the back of this.

This created what is known as "fiat money." Fiat money means that, for money to come into existence, the government simply prints some pieces of paper with nothing to back them up and declares that they are legal tender.

The word "fiat" comes from Latin and means an "arbitrary decree or pronouncement," so this does not exactly give you lots of confidence. In fact, these days, most fiat money does not even exist in paper form; it is simply created on computer screens.

Over the years, the fractional reserve ratio has become a lot more generous to the banks. In the USA, the ratio between lending and deposits is now typically 9:1. Around the world, the amount banks are required to hold in reserve can be even lower than 10%. In some cases, there is no limit on it at all. In the UK, there are no formal limits but a voluntary system is in place.

The overall effect is that banks are virtually free to simply create money out of thin air provided they work within the system and the limits laid down by governments.

In the USA, for example, it is estimated that less than 5% of the money supply actually exists as physical currency. Most simply exists on computer screens.

The following example gives an idea of how this works in practice. It shows how the banking system takes one deposit of just over £1,000 and turns it into loans worth almost £100,000 without any additional assets to back it up.

EXAMPLE:
HOW BANKS TURN A £1,000 DEPOSIT INTO £100,000 OF LOANS

- Joe goes to the bank because he wants a loan of £10,000 to buy a car.

- The bank he goes to is actually a new one and it doesn't even have any depositors yet. However, the bank's owners have deposited £1,112 of their own money with the central bank.

- Under the fractional reserve system, they are allowed to lend nine times the amount they have on deposit, so they can lend Joe his £10,000. They effectively invent the money by creating it in their computer systems and they credit it to his account.

- When he has been credited with the money, Joe writes a cheque for £10,000 to buy the car from Jill.

- Jill now deposits the £10,000 cheque in her bank account.

- Now Jill's bank has a new £10,000 that they can use for lending. However, they have to follow the fractional reserve requirement of 1:9 so they can lend £9,000 of it.

- Once they lend that £9,000 to someone else, it gets paid into that person's bank account and becomes the basis for a possible new loan of £8,100 (9 x £9,000).

- This process continues until, on the back of the original £1,112 deposited by the bank's owners, it is possible to lend almost £100,000.

In theory the situation described in the example could all happen within one bank. However, even when the money is deposited with several banks, it is all happening within the same system.

So, as a result of this process, we have almost £100,000 of debt created entirely on the back of one small deposit.

3

SIX INSIDER SECRETS OF BECOMING DEBT-FREE AND WEALTHY

The only real assets involved in this process are the ones being traded as a result of the loans, such as cars and houses. Meanwhile, the banks are profiting from interest on all these loans.

In practice, the banks will also have taken in some deposits from customers and will be paying out some interest to them—but naturally at much lower levels of interest than they are charging their borrowers.

Most people believe that when they borrow £10,000 from their bank, the bank has raised £10,000 to cover that. In fact, if the bank has raised £10,000, it could be using this to lend almost £100,000.

When they are allowed to charge interest on money they have created out of thin air, it's hardly surprising that banks make so much money. Later, we'll look in more detail at how banks make huge profits out of the interest they charge.

Later in this book I'll be showing you how to use a concept called "gearing" to copy the banks and turn your own £10,000 of cash into £100,000 asset. I'll show you how that principle can help you build your wealth much faster than would otherwise be possible.

 WEALTH WISDOM

The banking system is based on lending the same money many times. When banks and credit companies lend more to you, they can lend more to others and make higher profit. That is why they want you to borrow more. However, there is a way for you to copy that approach and build your own wealth faster.

WEALTH WORKOUT 4: FINANCIAL FREEDOM

List at least ten things you would do if you were financially free and had enough passive income to cover all your costs. For example, identify where you would live or what type of business you would set up or how you would spend your time.

1. _____

2. _____

3. _____

4. _____

5. _____

6. _____

7. _____

8. _____

9. _____

10. _____

3

SIX INSIDER SECRETS OF BECOMING DEBT-FREE AND WEALTHY

INSIDER WEALTH SECRET 3:
YOU CAN TURN THE WEALTH FLOW TOWARDS YOU

In the first secret, you saw how the choices you make every day affect the flow of wealth in your life and determine whether you end up wealthy or in debt.

In the second secret, you saw that money is not real and that the banks charge you over and over again for using the same money.

In this secret, you'll discover how to keep as much as possible of the wealth you already have in your life. You'll also find out how to use what you have to build extra wealth.

In other words, you'll learn how to make sure wealth flows into your personal Wealth Wheel instead of flowing out in the direction of banks, credit companies and other businesses.

The Incredible Power of Compound Growth

One of the most important factors to understand about the flow of wealth is COMPOUND GROWTH.

It is a concept that can either be a huge threat to your future wealth or a great opportunity, depending on how you use it.

The fact is, few people really understand the true power of compound growth yet it really is one of the most important keys to wealth.

It has been described as the Eighth Wonder of the World, and Einstein is even said to have claimed that it was the most powerful force in the universe.

I'm sure that many things have been described as the Eighth Wonder of the World and there is no real evidence that Einstein actually made that remark. Nevertheless neither comment exaggerates the importance of compound growth to your financial health.

Knowing about it is one of the keys to your wealth. You want to make sure it works in your favour instead of against you.

So what is compound growth?

Investopedia.com defines compounding as follows:

> The ability of an asset to generate earnings, which are then reinvested in order to generate their own earnings. In other words, compounding refers to generating earnings from previous earnings.

When it refers to interest, compounding simply means that once interest is added to your account, that same interest earns more interest in the future.

By the way, you'll notice that I refer to compound growth and compound interest. The concepts are the same—the only difference is that growth in value of a property, for example, is built into the value and not in the form of interest.

Here's how it works. If you put £1,000 in the bank and it earns 10% interest, at the end of a year, you will receive £100 of interest.

If you take that £100 out, you will still have £1,000 in the bank and you will earn £100 interest again the following year. This will continue indefinitely as long as interest rates don't change and you don't touch the capital.

However, with compound interest, if you leave the £100 in the account, during the following year you will earn interest on £1,100—meaning that at the end of the year you will get £110 in interest.

If you leave that in the account, then next year, you will earn interest on £1,210.

The same thing applies to the value of an asset. For example if you buy a property for £100,000 and it grows in value by 10% a year, it will be worth £110,000 the second year, then £121,100 the following year and so on. The growth becomes part of the value and also shares in the future growth.

MASTER YOUR MINDSET

Compound growth simply means that your money can earn money all by itself—it requires no "work" from you!

The thing is, because the amounts involved are usually relatively small year to year, most people don't realise just how significant the impact of compound interest or compound growth can be over a period of years.

However, compound growth is rather like that snowball rolling downhill we talked about in the introduction. It may start out pretty small but, once it picks up some pace, it can grow in size very quickly and end up making a big impact.

The decisions you make about how you spend your money will determine whether it works in your favour or against you.

Here are a couple of stories that illustrate what a big mistake it is to underestimate the power of compound growth and compound interest.

The Price of Manhattan

People often laugh when they hear the story that the island of Manhattan was sold by the local Lenape Indians to a Dutch trader in exchange for some beads worth sixty guilders (about $24).

The exact truth of this story is hard to determine but it does prove the point very well.

The question is whether that would have been a good deal in 1626. After all, it seems a tiny price to pay for what is now some of the world's most valuable real estate.

If that $24 had been invested at 8% interest, compounded annually for 385 years (1626-2011), it would have grown to a staggering...

$164 Trillion!

Yes, you read it right, not million or billion, but trillion.

Are you beginning to see the power of compound growth?

Two Thrifty Sisters

As another way of illustrating this, there is also the story of two twin sisters.

- One started saving £2,000 a year when she was eighteen. She kept doing this for only twelve years—until she was thirty—and then stopped paying in. So she paid in a total of £24,000. However, she left the money invested and it continued to build up until she retired at age sixty-five.

- Meanwhile the other sister started saving the same amount at age thirty and continued making the payments every year until age sixty-five. She paid into her account for thirty-five years, a total of £70,000.

Both of them earned the same rate of interest—8% compound. Which do you think would have more at age sixty-five?

Most people would guess it was the second sister but it's actually the first. At age sixty-five:

- The first sister had £561,167 in her account.
- The second sister had £344,634 in her account.

The first sister not only ended up with a fund worth £216,533 more, she actually paid in £46,000 less than her sister!

The difference clearly shows the astonishing power of compound interest over time.

THE RULE OF 70

There is a very useful shorthand approach that allows you to get some idea of the power of compound growth or interest without needing to have an accountant or a scientific calculator handy. It's called the Rule of 70 and here's how it works.

$$T = 70/x$$

T is the length of time it takes your investment to double and x is the % compound rate of interest you earn. For example, if you invest £1,000 at 7% per year compound interest, it will double in value in 10 years.

$$T = 70/7 = 10$$

Another way of looking at this is that, your £1,000 would half in value over 20 years if inflation was 3.5%.

You may see this referred to as the Rule of 72 in places as the exact number depends on the compounding and some people feel 72 is easier to use for calculations. 70 usually gives you a more accurate result.

Turning Compound Growth to Your Advantage

So the key point about compound interest is that it has a big impact on how wealth flows.

- When you are paying interest or you buy something that reduces in value, wealth is flowing **away** from you.
- When you earn interest or you buy something that increases in value, wealth is flowing **towards** you.

So compound growth or compound interest is a wonderful concept—when it works in your favour. But the problem is that when you are paying the interest instead of earning it, you are losing out big time.

If you are behind on loan or credit card payments—or your payments are less than the monthly interest due—you can end up paying interest on the interest you owe, which increases your outlays significantly.

Why do you think the credit industry always wants you to spend more? It's a siphon draining your financial life away.

You have to turn compound growth to your advantage. It's time to stop wasting money to make credit card companies rich!

Instead of paying interest, you should start earning interest and enjoying the benefits of compound growth.

When you let compound growth work against you, it's like looking through a telescope the wrong way—it makes your Wealth Wheel smaller and puts your financial freedom much further into the future.

So turn the telescope around the correct way, share in the benefits of compound growth and start making your Wealth Wheel bigger.

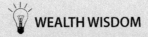 **WEALTH WISDOM**

Compound interest is where your interest earns interest. Where you make this work in your favour—through your investments—you can turn relatively small amounts into large amounts faster than you'd believe possible. If it is working against you—through your debts—small amounts quickly become very large.

How Banks Can Make 1000% Profit or More on Your Debts

One of the main places your wealth goes when it flows away from you is into the coffers of the banks and credit companies.

When you borrow money, you expect your bank to charge you interest until you pay back the loan. But you may not realise just how much profit this interest will make them.

One of the ways banks secure funds to enable them to lend to you is that they borrow money from other banks.

The rate at which banks can borrow is determined by the minimum rate set by the central bank, which in the case of the UK is the Bank of England.

The rate at which banks lend to and borrow from one another is linked to this and in the UK is known as Libor—the London Interbank Offered Rate. Libor is used as the reference rate for many other currencies, while the Euribor is used in the Eurozone.

Often when you borrow money, the rate will be fixed as a certain percentage over this rate, which will be higher than the central bank base rate.

So, for example, when the Bank of England base rate is 1%, the Libor rate may be 2%. Consumer mortgages, for example, may be set at 1% over Libor.

Therefore, if the Libor rate is 2%, the mortgage rate could be 3%. (The actual mortgage rate paid depends on a huge range of factors but this keeps the example simple.)

3

The bank is effectively borrowing money at 2% and lending it to you at 3%. You might expect that this 1% margin is where they make their money. And you'd be right. Well, partly right.

Because if you are thinking their profit on that transaction is 1%, you may be shocked to discover the truth. The bank is making more. Much more!

The bank makes a profit of 50%: The difference between the 2% they pay and the 3% they get from you is 50% profit to them.

Let's work that through:

- You want to borrow £100,000.
- The bank borrows this at 2% interest, so they pay £2,000 a year as the cost of borrowing.
- You pay the bank 3% interest, or £3,000 a year, as your cost of borrowing.
- The bank pockets £1,000 profit for selling a product that costs them £2,000 to acquire.

Pretty good business for them!

Of course they do have some costs to pay but they will probably have included some charges when you took out the loan and there is a pretty fat margin in that profit to cover their costs.

Now here is the really shocking part. The interest rates of most loans and credit cards are much higher than for mortgages. A typical credit card rate can easily be over 20%.

So when the bank is charging you 20% on your credit card debt and paying only 2% for the money, they are raking in profits of close to 1,000%.

How good does that make you feel?

Can you see why the bank was so keen to give you a credit card and lend you money?

Believe it or not, they are not done yet. As I explained in the previous section, the bank can actually lend part of the same money over and over so they can multiply their profit many times.

At the same time, the bank may be paying you between 1% and 3% interest on your savings if you are lucky.

Have you ever wondered why banks manage to make so much money even in tough times?

Well, now you know.

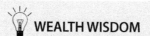

WEALTH WISDOM

Banks borrow money from each other at relatively low rates and then lend it to you in the form of credit card debt at very high rates. They may well be making around 1,000% profit or more on the money you owe them on your credit cards.

Inflation

Another way in which wealth flows away from you is when its value is eaten away by inflation. Inflation is caused when prices increase so that the spending power of the penny in your pocket is reduced.

In the 1970s and 1980s, high inflation rates ate away significantly at the value of savings. But, for much of the 1990s and early 2000s, it ceased to be a problem and many people almost forgot about it.

However, it became an issue again in the recent global financial crisis.

At this point, the issue became even worse, raising the spectre of "stagflation," where price increases are not matched by economic growth. This means prices rise but earnings do not—so wealth is depleted.

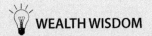 **WEALTH WISDOM**

Inflation is back and it is eating away at the value of any savings you have. There are now more things to buy, they cost more, and your money buys you less every day.

The Pension Problem

Another place in our lives where wealth flows away from us tends to be retirement.

The strange thing is that people seem to accept this is normal. After a lifetime of work, we expect to have to downsize our lives and have fewer pleasures.

Somehow, people think they will have significantly lower costs in retirement. In fact, it rarely turns out like this.

These days, you can expect to live quite a long time in retirement, enjoying relatively good health. Whether through choice or otherwise, you will probably also have a lot of leisure time and many things you would like to do.

> **MASTER YOUR MINDSET**
>
> Financial freedom is the ability to live the lifestyle you desire without having to work or rely on anyone else for money.

It's therefore unrealistic to think you won't need a good level of income to be able to enjoy a good lifestyle.

However, the reality is that many people end up cutting their expenditure as they simply don't have enough money.

So, if you are still hanging hopefully on to the idea that somebody else will take care of you in retirement, there are some important facts you need to know. To put it quite simply the numbers just don't add up.

For the twenty years or so after the end of the Second World War, there was an unusual spike in the birth rate in many countries. The birth rate had been subdued both by the war and by the Great Depression which preceded it.

The people who were born in this period actually became known as the baby boomers and this is the generation that is currently approaching or already in retirement.

3

SIX INSIDER SECRETS OF BECOMING DEBT-FREE AND WEALTHY

This generation have generally done pretty well financially compared to previous generations and they had a lot of money to spend. But in general they have not saved very much and they also didn't have as many children as their parents did.

Why is this important?

Well, most state pension schemes were set up as a safety net to ensure people didn't suffer poverty in retirement. They were set up at a time when the population was growing and they are generally funded on a pay-as-you-go basis, which means the pensions to people who have retired are paid by those still actively working.

The exact numbers vary from country to country but, at the start, typically two or three active members were paying for one person's pension.

Here is the problem. Birth rates have declined significantly and people are living longer than before. As a result, we have more people in retirement and fewer people working. The balance has changed.

There are now significantly fewer people in work sharing the burden of the growing cost of retirement benefits.

The only options that will allow the system to continue are:

- Paying lower pensions to people when they retire.
- Making the people still working pay higher contributions (though why should they do this, as it is not for their benefit?).

- Working for longer and retiring later (as people are healthier and will generally live longer than before, this may be a good option).

However, the system is arguably unsustainable and you can't rule out the possibility of complete collapse.

The situation with company pension schemes is even more striking. Many large businesses set up pension schemes when they had more than ten employees for every pensioner.

Demographic and economic changes mean that the situation is now more likely to be the other way around. Company pension schemes are therefore either closing down or becoming significantly less generous.

That doesn't mean that state and employer pensions shouldn't play a part in planning your future. It does mean you need to make your own savings and investment plans in addition to state and company pensions. The alternative is quite simply poverty in retirement.

When it comes to private pensions, the value you'll get depends on how well your money has been looked after—and what charges you have to pay. The truth is many people investing in private pension plans end up disappointed—having much less than they expected, especially when inflation begins to take its toll.

If you're relying on your children (or everybody else's) to keep funding your needs in old age, it's time to face the reality.

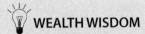

WEALTH WISDOM

The cost of the traditional system of providing retirement pensions is becoming unsustainable as fewer people are in the workforce and people are living longer.

How Wealth Affects Your Health and Relationships

One of the most distressing aspects of seeing people's wealth flow away from them in debt interest is the immense impact it has on the things that most of us view as most important in life—health and family.

Too often I've seen strong relationships founder on the back of struggling to maintain a normal life under the burden of debt—even though there is almost always a solution that would see the problem disappear in a relatively short time.

Too many times I have seen people suffering various degrees of ill health due to the worry and stress of financial problems.

The extent of the problem was revealed in a study by The Consumer Credit Counselling Service, a UK charity. Here are some of the highlights of the survey:

- 83% said debt problems had a very negative impact on their lives.
- 37% said debt problems had adversely affected their relationship with their partner.
- 46% said debt problems had a very negative impact on their health.
- 65% said debt problems had a negative impact on their ability to do their job.

It's clear from studies like this that debt creates a vicious circle of problems.

Relationship Problems

People are often reluctant to discuss financial worries with their partners and this can lead to ongoing problems.

Financial problems in a relationship may arise because the two people have very different attitudes to money. One may be very cautious while the other is spendthrift.

Though many couples these days have their own separate accounts and financial needs, it's still common for one half of the partnership to be the one that looks after the money.

This can often mean that joint finances run into serious difficulties without one half knowing anything about it.

On the other hand, it's quite common for two people in a relationship both to run up separate debts and then find the problems multiply when they are combined.

> **MASTER YOUR MINDSET**
>
> In a relationship, it's important to be open about money issues.

People are reluctant to discuss their finances with others at the best of times and this becomes even more so when problems arise. The CCCS survey showed that only about a third of respondents had discussed their financial problems with their partners.

Relationship problems—especially divorce—can also be a major cause of financial difficulties.

Health Concerns

In the survey, the range of health problems people attributed to their finances was very varied including nervous breakdown, loss of hair, palpitations, and cessation of menstruation.

Less than 10% of people said debt problems had no effect on their health.

Financial problems impacted people's ability to do their work in various ways. Many reported that the constant worry about debt made it difficult to concentrate at times and others said they were left with no money for basic expenses such as the cost of petrol or travelling to work.

One way to highlight the constant stress people endure when facing debt problems is to recognize the immense relief people feel when they find a way out of their debt problems.

Here are just a few of the ways people say their lives have changed when they get completely out of debt:

- "I look forward to the mail arriving."
- "An unexpected bill doesn't cause me any worries."
- "I am no longer worried every time the telephone rings."
- "I have a better relationship with my partner as we no longer fight about money."
- "I feel better about being able to pay bills when they arrive rather than have them hanging over me for weeks."
- "I have cut down on my working hours as I don't need the extra cash anymore."
- "I can finally sleep at night!"

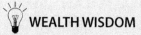

WEALTH WISDOM

Money problems are the single biggest cause or relationship problems and can be a major cause of stress and health problems. Solving money worries can therefore improve your health and your relationships.

WEALTH WORKOUT 5: THE WEALTH FLOW

List some of the factors in your financial life that cause wealth to flow away from you such as interest you pay on debts or things you have bought that are reducing in value.

Now list some of the factors in your financial life that allow wealth to flow towards you such as interest you earn or things you have bought that are increasing in value.

Note any problems you have had in your health or relationships that could be down to money.

3

SIX INSIDER SECRETS OF BECOMING DEBT-FREE AND WEALTHY

INSIDER WEALTH SECRET 4:
DEBT CAN BE GOOD OR BAD

As we have seen already, the key to achieving wealth and financial freedom is the size of your Wealth Wheel.

There are three ways to *increase* the size of your wealth wheel.

1. Increasing your income.
2. Reducing your expenditure.
3. Owning things that increase in value.

Equally, there are three ways to *reduce* the size of your wealth wheel.

1. Reducing your income.
2. Increasing your expenditure.
3. Owning things that reduce in value.

Later in this book, we'll be looking at steps you can take to increase your income. And in the next chapter, we'll focus on various steps you can take to reduce your spending.

One of most important measures of wealth—the size of your Wealth Wheel—is what's called NET WORTH. The keys to understanding net worth are assets and liabilities. At the most simple level:

· An **asset** is something you **own**.
· A **liability** is something you **owe**.

So your assets might include your house, stocks and shares you own, any investment property or valuables such as paintings.

These are the key components that determine the size of your Wealth Wheel.

On the other hand, your liabilities would be your debts such as your mortgage, credit card debts and other loans. So the size of your Wealth Wheel—your net worth—is determined by the following formula:

Your Net Worth = What You Own—What You Owe

The less you owe, the more you own and the bigger your Wealth Wheel as shown below. Obviously the ideal situation is to reduce the size of the inner wheel as fast as possible so that you owe nothing.

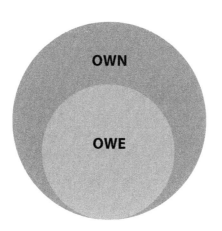

Let's look at a real example of net worth. If you know somebody owns the following assets, they may *appear* wealthy.

Assets	(£)
Home	400,000
Cars	25,000
Investments	5,000
Total	**430,000**

They have assets of £430,000. But the picture changes when you look at what they owe—their debts.

Debts	(£)
Home Mortgage	(190,000)
Car Loans	(12,000)
Other Loans	(26,000)
Credit Cards	(9,000)
Total	**(237,000)**

They have debts of £237,000 so you have to put the two together to get the real picture of their net worth.

	Assets	Debts	Net Value
Home	400,000	(190,000)	210,000
Cars	25,000	(12,000)	13,000
Loans	-	(26,000)	(26,000)
Credit cards	-	(9,000)	(9,000)
Investments	5,000	-	5,000
Total	**430,000**	**(237,000)**	**193,000**

The true picture of their net worth is therefore less than £200,000. The best way to build their net worth is therefore to get rid of the debt as soon as possible.

So part of the key to building the biggest Wealth Wheel possible is owning as much as possible, while owing as little as possible.

However, there are a couple of additional considerations.

Only Some Assets Build Wealth

In calculating your Net Worth, anything you own is considered to be an asset. So, if you own a car or a boat, for example, you should consider them assets for the purposes of your net worth calculation.

However, in his best-selling *Rich Dad, Poor Dad* series, Robert Kiyosaki makes an important additional point about assets and liabilities.

He says we need to think about whether the assets that we own have the potential to increase our wealth or reduce it. So he makes a stricter definition. He says:

Double

- An **asset** is something you own that either increases in value or generates income.
- A **liability** is something that costs you money.

You could say that assets make you richer while liabilities make you poorer. So we need to think about whether the assets we own have the potential to increase our wealth or reduce it.

MASTER YOUR MINDSET

To expand your wealth zone, you have to step out of your comfort zone.

For example, if you own a car, it has a value but it is also a continual drain on your income as you have a steady stream of bills such as petrol, repairs, and insurance.

In addition, your car is declining in value all the time—quite significantly in the early years. Owning a car therefore reduces your wealth so has to be counted as a liability from that viewpoint.

Liabilities are therefore anything that consumes your monthly income and reduces the size of your Wealth Wheel.

Suppose on the other hand that one of your assets is a small flat that you let out to tenants. Certainly it involves some costs that you have to pay but hopefully these are more than covered by the rental income you receive. Over time, it should also increase in value.

This is a true wealth-building asset.

So a wealth-building asset is something you own that pays you an income or that grows in value with the intention that you can sell it and capture the value.

When I get you to list and value your assets in the next section, I will ask you to separate wealth-producing assets from other assets. So you would count investment property as a wealth-producing asset but your car will be listed under other assets.

You may notice that your bank will count your car as an asset if you apply for a loan but that's because it's something they can repossess and sell if you owe them money.

So, if you have loans, what you think of as your assets may really be assets of the bank.

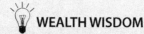

WEALTH WISDOM

Wealth-building assets increase in value or generate income. Liabilities reduce in value or cost you money.

Good Debt and Bad Debt

One of the reasons why this distinction is important is that it helps us make decisions about debt.

I've been busy running down the banks and credit cards companies and you may think I've got a personal issue about the idea of debt. Let me be clear, there are two types of debt and there is a big difference between them.

- **Good Debt:** This is debt you use to acquire an asset which generates an income and/or increases in value. Ideally the income you earn from owning the asset more than covers the cost of repaying the loan. This could apply when you own an investment property, for example.

- **Bad Debt:** This is a debt that is used to acquire something that reduces in value or costs you money. This would include most credit card debt, car loans, or loans for things like holidays.

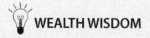

WEALTH WISDOM

Good debt is used to buy something that generates income or increases in value. Bad debt buys something that reduces in value or costs you money.

Here's something to bear in mind though. The fact that debt can be defined as "good" doesn't mean that it's a good thing to hang on to it.

The distinction is mainly to help you decide whether to take out a loan for this purpose. Once you have a good debt, you still want to get the best terms possible for the loan and then usually pay it off as soon as possible.

Where you have a "good" debt that has a higher interest rate than a "bad" debt, you may even want to pay off the good debt first.

Is Your Own Home An Asset?

On the basis of what I've said so far, you might be wondering whether you should safely consider your own home to be an asset—and whether we would consider your home mortgage to be a good debt or a bad debt.

> **MASTER YOUR MINDSET**
>
> Owning your own home may not always be the best way to accumulate wealth.

After all, we're always being told by the "experts" that owning your own home is a major "investment" and many people therefore try to buy the biggest home possible.

Strictly, on the *Rich Dad Poor Dad* definition, your home is a liability because, even when your mortgage is paid off, your home is a drain on your monthly income.

If you really plan to sell off your home and move to something smaller or cheaper, your home may be helping to build your future wealth. Many people start out with that intention but it doesn't always work out that way.

A home that is too big or too expensive can become a major millstone. There are many better ways to build wealth than buying a bigger home. We'll cover these in more detail later.

Nevertheless, in most situations, I believe it's a good idea for most people to buy the home they live in and most people will need to borrow money to do that.

You want to get to a stage where you can live with very few outgoings and therefore owning your own home is usually better than paying rent.

The keys are that you should buy a property that is right for your long-term needs and you should focus on paying off the mortgage as soon as possible.

WEALTH WORKOUT 6: GOOD DEBT AND BAD DEBT

List all of your debts—including your mortgage and credit cards—and categorise them as "good" or "bad."

Debts	(£)	Good Debt	Bad Debt
Mortgage			
Other home loans			
Credit card balances			
Other loans			
Other debts			
Total			

Good Debt

INSIDER WEALTH SECRET 5:
THERE IS A CONSPIRACY TO MAKE YOU SPEND MORE

The biggest issue that causes most people to get into debt is that we face a concerted campaign to "steal" our money.

Ranged against you are the combined forces of the retailers, the manufacturers and the credit companies. They are in business to make money and so they want to take it out of your pocket.

It's all perfectly legal but they will do it by convincing you to buy something you don't really need and can't afford right now. They use whatever tools are necessary to get you to buy more stuff.

The advertising campaigns—supported by articles in the media— are full of pretty pictures that promise to make you just like the happy people in the picture if only you buy what they are selling.

They are experts at making you desire what they are selling and then they will persuade you to buy.

They Need Us to Take Action and Buy

The advertisers' mantra is AIDA—they strive to create Awareness, Interest, Desire, and Action.

The action they want is you taking out your wallet and buying. And they want you to buy right now—they know if you think about it you'll talk yourself out of it.

No money? No problem! They—or their friends the credit card providers—will happily lend it to you.

If they can't persuade you to buy directly, they'll enlist your family and friends to persuade you. It's what we call "Keeping up with Joneses."

What happens is that people become poor because they give away their wealth trying to look well off. However, they could have invested their money instead and they could actually be genuinely wealthy.

Taking Responsibility

One of the first steps to getting out of debt is to admit that you are 100% responsible for where you are and where you are going. You can't change things if you don't take responsibility.

You need to stop allowing yourself to be brainwashed.

That means realising that credit is nothing more than a ploy to steal your money and trade it for some low-value experience or product that you probably don't really want.

> **MASTER YOUR MINDSET**
>
> You should control your financial future—not an advertiser!

You should think of most advertising and promotion as being just like a thief coming in your bedroom window.

The belief that buying things will make you feel better is a thought that has been planted by others.

What is going on in your mind will determine your wealth. So, if you allow others to control your mind, they will control your wealth.

You have got into debt by thinking the way advertisers have programmed you to think.

They call us "consumers" and the word "consume" literally means "waste, squander, destroy totally."

We are indoctrinated to consume to help others prosper.

This is how some people earn more than £1 million during their lives and end up with nothing in the bank.

They get talked in to giving all their wealth away to manufacturers, retailers and credit card companies because they thought it would make them feel better or impress the neighbours.

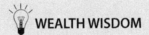 **WEALTH WISDOM**

Every day we face an alliance of manufacturers, retailers and credit providers who need our money and will do everything possible to make us part with it. We need to resist this manipulation.

Money is Emotional

You might think that all the numbers and all the statistics would make issues to do with money very rational and planned.

In fact the exact opposite is true. Most of the choices we make about money are rooted in our emotions.

Money seems to be able to trigger virtually every human emotion and often triggers many at the same time.

Psychologists say that the emotions most often triggered by money (in order of importance) are Anxiety, Depression, Anger, Helplessness, Happiness, Excitement, Envy, and Resentment. These emotions influence our behaviour significantly:

- We want everything now.
- We want what others have.
- We buy to feel good.

Let's look at these points in more detail.

We Want Everything Now

One of the advantages of modern life is that we can have most things we want almost instantly.

Information is at our fingertips on the internet; food is available either in minutes off the shelf or ready to pop in the microwave; books can be downloaded online and virtually everything can be delivered to our door.

We are used to everything being instantly and easily available. So why wait until we can afford it? We can acquire now and pay later.

The problem is that it's so easy to make purchases that we make them too quickly and often regret them later.

> **MASTER YOUR MINDSET**
>
> Impulse purchases almost always turn out to be the ones you regret.

Brian was a gadget enthusiast and always wanted to be the first of his friends to have the latest gimmick. He was pretty pleased with himself because he always spent a lot of time researching the best-value products and searching the internet for the lowest prices.

But he was pretty shocked when he realised that he had spent over £3,500 in the last few months and almost everything was now out of date.

That experience is far from unusual. Just think about a few things you have bought in the last year or two and regretted afterwards!

> **MASTER YOUR MINDSET**
>
> When we buy on credit, we pay a premium that the bank puts in its pocket.

Here's the reality. You ended up with junk; the banks and credit card companies got your money. You may have felt good for a short time but that feeling probably didn't last long and was most likely replaced with regret.

This is a common psychological response after buying things. The marketing gurus call it "buyer's remorse" and for many larger purchases, they will have a strategy in place to make sure you don't change your mind once you have bought.

They don't want you asking for your money back.

It may seem a harsh comparison but using your credit card and spending money is, in many ways, like being addicted to drugs. It is all about seeking short-term gratification and then we want more and it stores up long-term problems.

When we buy on credit, we want the benefits now and forget we have to pay the bills later. Using credit can appear to enhance your lifestyle but soon becomes a ball and chain as paying off the debt drags you down.

The Power of Instant Gratification

There was a fascinating study at Stanford University in 1972 where a group of children were left in a room with a marshmallow and told they would be given a second one if they resisted eating the first while the adult was out..

In a series of follow-up studies, it was discovered that children who were able to defer gratification were actually more successful in several aspects of life than those who wanted instant gratification.

The fact is that sometimes it's better to be able to wait than to have what you want right now. Being able to buy what you want may make you feel wealthy but, when the bill arrives, the reality is that you are not.

One simple way to get off this instant gratification treadmill is to get into the habit of waiting a week or so before buying something you think you want. Most of the time, you'll wonder why you even considered it in the first place.

The same argument applies if you are selling something. Often we make decisions to sell based on fear. Somebody makes an offer for your house and you are worried you won't get a better deal so you end up selling for too little.

The way to handle this is to make sure you get advice from two or more experts before you make a decision to sell.

3

SIX INSIDER SECRETS OF BECOMING DEBT-FREE AND WEALTHY

True wealth is more often achieved by the tortoise than by the hare. It may seem like a challenge to wait a little longer but it usually leads to better results.

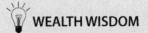

WEALTH WISDOM

Before buying or selling something, wait at least a week before doing anything. If it's a big decision, ask advice from at least one expert.

We Want What Others Have (Keeping Up with the Joneses)

The biggest reason most people get into debt is that they want to look and feel as if they are better off than they really are.

And one of the biggest factors forcing them to do that is that they want to feel they are keeping pace with their friends and neighbours. Certain possessions and activities become essential because other people are buying them or doing them.

Jim and Rosie stretched themselves financially to add an extension on their house just like the one their neighbours had. They didn't realise that the neighbours had come into an inheritance that had enabled them to pay for it.

Instead Jim and Rosie added it to their mortgage and then bought a large-screen TV on their credit card to add to the new room.

They didn't really need the extra room but at least they felt good because they were keeping up with the neighbours.

The problem with this concept—which we call "Keeping Up with the Joneses"—is that the Joneses are very often on the wrong road.

You think they are having fun but they are going broke.

When your friends are always making new purchases, you don't really know if they have saved up the money, have won the lottery, or are already way overstretched on the credit card.

It all starts early—kids want something because their friends have it and parents are under immense pressure to give in.

A few years ago, the things kids wanted may have seemed quite costly but the cost then was nothing compared to what they want today.

What kind of lesson is it giving to kids that everything they want is easily available and they just need to ask and they can get it?

If you keep on thinking that people will like you more because you drive a big car and wear more expensive clothes, you will end up poor.

On the other hand if you stop caring what other people think and make your own choices, you'll be better placed to buy what you want.

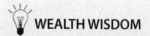

WEALTH WISDOM

Never buy something based on what other people own. You never know their true financial situation and they may be running into serious problems. Buy based on what you want, need, and can afford.

We Buy To Feel Good

People joke about the term "therapy shopping"—you've had a hard week at the office so you buy a new jacket on Saturday to make you feel better.

This type of impulse buying is a serious problem and its chief cause is stress. We think the purchase is going to make us feel better but it rarely does. It may provide a quick rush but the reality is that these purchases are often storing up real stress for later when the bills come in.

When you have racked up a few grand on the credit card and are struggling to make the repayments, then you really are stressed.

The other way that psychology drives our purchases is that we often buy things that we think will make others like us. This can be anything from buying expensive cologne that we think makes us more attractive to buying a new car that is supposed to make people like you more.

It's crazy but true—and it doesn't work.

Nothing you buy will make you more attractive, more popular or more successful.

Whatever psychological fulfilment you thought you were buying, you didn't get it and you just wasted your money.

People see ability to buy what they want as part of who they are and credit is an important part of that.

But credit only does one thing—it makes everything cost more. You're not just paying the price—you're paying the price plus interest. You can't afford to let your self-image get tied up with your spending habits.

People who look like they have a lot of money have often wasted all their money trying to look that way. The people who don't look like they have a lot of money often don't look it because they haven't wasted money for the sake of appearances.

Remember that distinction I made between Wealth Accumulators and Consumers:

- **Wealth accumulators** live as if they earn half of what they really do. They end up rich and can enjoy anything they like.
- **Consumers** behave as if they earn twice as much as they really do but they end up poor and working in their retirement years.

If you ever find yourself thinking that buying something will make you feel better, it's time to put your credit card away. If you want to get wealthy, learn to recognize your moods and make sure they don't affect your behaviour.

Never go shopping when you feel stressed or unhappy. If you find yourself going shopping for fun or to cheer yourself up, it's time to get a new hobby instead.

If you go shopping with friends for social reasons, perhaps you should find a better way to spend time with them.

3

SIX INSIDER SECRETS OF BECOMING DEBT-FREE AND WEALTHY

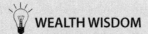

WEALTH WISDOM

Think very carefully about your reasons for buying something. If you think it will make you feel better or make others like you more, find another reason.

WEALTH WORKOUT 7: THE CONSUMPTION CONSPIRACY

Draw up a list of some things you have bought over the last three years that you regretted afterwards.

Item	Reason bought	Times used	Cost

SIX INSIDER SECRETS OF BECOMING DEBT-FREE AND WEALTHY

3

INSIDER WEALTH SECRET 6:
WEALTHY PEOPLE THINK DIFFERENTLY

One of the biggest reasons people run into problems with money is that few of us are fortunate enough to grow up in an environment where we are comfortable with it.

We are never taught how it works and, as a result, it exerts a control over us that is difficult to shake off.

This can put us at a huge disadvantage so there are many changes we need to make in the way we think and behave if we want to be wealthy. Here are five steps you need to take:

1. Commit to financial education.
2. Challenge your beliefs about money.
3. Change your wealth thermostat setting.
4. Connect to your own wealth personality.
5. Choose advisers who know how to create wealth.

1. Commit to Financial Education

It's hardly surprising that so many people become victims of debt and money problems because hardly anybody has the benefit of genuine financial education.

Our education system is not set up to teach people about how money works and, to the extent that information is made available, it is usually promoted by people who have strong vested interests.

You may learn how to work out the interest on your mortgage but who is going to explain to you how much it really costs?

Who is going to tell you that paying off your mortgage sooner will save you a lot of money—certainly not your bank!

This leads to the problem that we are not only badly informed about how the financial system works to our disadvantage, we don't even realise the degree to which this is true.

Our knowledge and habits related to money typically come from our parents and other family and friends.

However the financial world has moved so fast over the last thirty years that habits and knowledge from our parents' generation are almost irrelevant to the way we live today.

Having said that, the sad reality is that many of the principles that the previous generations followed are actually more relevant in today's debt-laden society than ever. But they need to be updated to reflect modern life.

I know that, in my own experience, growing up, I wasn't in an environment where I was learning about finances and how to handle large amounts of money. But I did grow up recognising the value of money and knowing that hard-earned cash should not be thrown away lightly.

Some of the lessons we could learn from our parents' generation about only buying what you can afford and keeping life simple would be extremely valuable to us today.

Many wealthy people are lucky enough to grow up understanding some of the realities of money. That doesn't necessarily mean they grew up with lots of money. Often not having money helps people respect it more and therefore build for the future more effectively.

The good news is that it is always possible to make up for the poor start you got in your financial education by investing in it now. Time spent attending seminars, reading books or listening to audio training will be well rewarded in your future wealth.

The truth is that your financial education is one of the most important investments you can make in your future wealth.

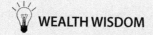

WEALTH WISDOM

Improving your financial knowledge through education is one of the most important investments you can make in your future wealth.

2. Challenge Your Beliefs about Money

Most of us develop ideas about money quite early on and, unless we are very lucky, these beliefs can hold us back later in life.

Very often we are influenced by negative emotions about money that affect how we spend, earn and invest.

These negative emotions are often at a fairly unconscious level and may not always be expressed directly but they can have a big effect on the way people think and behave.

For example, if you are used to hearing that someone who is wealthy has probably done something illegal, or hasn't worked hard or is just lucky, you easily develop the unconscious idea that only bad people become wealthy.

Who wants to be wealthy if that means others will think of you as bad?

When you hear that only lucky people become rich, you'll never believe that you too can have financial freedom.

If you want to achieve financial freedom, you need to start thinking about where you got your ideas about money and maybe you will need to challenge some of them.

Developing the right mindset for wealth is really a whole field on its own. I recommend taking time to study books such as:
- *Secrets of the Millionaire Mind* by T. Harv Eker
- *The Richest Man in Babylon* by George S. Clason

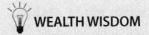 WEALTH WISDOM

The attitudes and habits we develop about money in our early days can affect us for the rest of our lives. Often it requires a conscious effort to change the way you think and behave.

3. Change Your Wealth Thermostat Setting

Another issue related to the psychology of money that holds many people back is that people get used to having a certain amount of money and find it difficult to think outside that box.

This is rather like the thermostat on your water heater, but when it comes to wealth, this thermostat is faulty for most people.

In your water heater, the thermostat stops the water going over a certain temperature. Having this kind of restriction on your finances can prevent you going beyond a certain level of income.

It doesn't matter whether it is £10,000 a year or £100,000 a year, if you get used to earning a certain amount, you might find it difficult to push your income above that level.

Your thermostat may be set by your conditioning when you were young, by your friends and family, or by your own limiting beliefs. But it can be a major restriction on your earning potential.

Ironically, a faulty thermostat has the opposite effect on your spending power. It doesn't place any limit at all.

For many people, this means an unexpected cash windfall is immediately seen as extra spending power.

And the real risk is that they feel rich when they get an increase in the limit on their credit card. They immediately think they have more money.

The key problem for many people is that they think of their credit card limit as part of their income and they spend it every month.

Wealthy people know exactly how much money they need to spend every month to cover their important outgoings.

Anything above that limit—and any new income—is applied first to debt repayment or to building an emergency fund. Then they make investment a priority, with any luxury purchases budgeted or carefully considered.

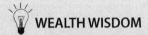

WEALTH WISDOM

Your wealth thermostat is an unconscious control that can stop you growing your income above a certain level or it can make you spend too much. You may need to adjust it if you want to be wealthy.

4. Connect to Your Own Wealth Personality

People handle money in different ways according to what type of personality they are.

Some people are lucky enough to be wired with the type of personality that makes them get better results with money, while others have their work cut out because they are not wired for success.

However, it's often not about being wired the wrong way or the right way; it's about knowing yourself and getting the best results possible based on who you are.

Psychologist Adrian Furnham—who helped create the *Big Money Test* series for the BBC—categorises people in the following way according to how they manage their finances:

- **Misers** fear becoming penniless and have trouble enjoying the benefits of their money.
- **Spenders** shop in an often uncontrolled manner, particularly when feeling low—and get a short-lived high, often followed by guilt.

- **Tycoons** see money as a route to power and approval, and believe wealth will make them happy.
- **Bargain hunters** feel superior when they get discounts, and feel angry if expected to pay full price.
- **Gamblers** feel exhilarated when taking chances, and find it hard to stop—even when losing—as a win brings a sense of power.

Virtually all personality types can face problems when it comes to dealing with money, especially when they have to think about planning and budgeting for the future.

Even those who are organised may not make the best out of their finances because they may hold back from investing for the future.

One vital key to taking control of your finances is knowing what kind of financial manager you are.

You may not be able to change your personality but knowing yourself better helps you to work around it and make changes where you can.

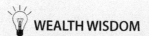 **WEALTH WISDOM**

Get to know what type of financial personality you are so that you know how best to build your wealth strategy.

5. Choose Advisers Who Know How to Create Wealth

With all these challenges around the topic of money, it would be good to think there was somewhere we could go for help. The problem is that most of us trust the wrong people. In fact, the reality is that most of us don't even talk to anyone.

Part of the big issue around money is that people don't like to talk about it—least of all when they have problems. They don't discuss it with their partners as they want to avoid a fight. They don't discuss it with their friends as they don't want to be making comparisons.

You can compare the situation of financial advice to looking for medical help. If you are ill, you go to a doctor and if you have a specific problem, you want help from someone who is a specialist in that area.

However, with financial problems, people often don't know who they can trust. Indeed, often they don't even realise they have a problem. So, if they go anywhere at all for help and advice, where do they go?

The big problem is that most people go for advice from people who have the same problems as they do.

They get financial advice from someone who works for a bank and is also overburdened with debt.

Or they get tips from reading the newspapers that are financed by advertising from the companies that caused their problems in the first place.

Instead they should be getting advice from someone who is suitably qualified to help in their situation.

In the case of someone with financial problems, that may be a local Citizens Advice Bureau in the UK or a similar independent body in other countries.

But when it comes to building wealth, people often go to financial advisers who are making a living based on earning a salary and fees or commission for giving advice.

Quite often these are people who have similar financial worries and problems to themselves. Why would you take advice about financial freedom from someone who depends on their pay cheque every month?

Financial advisers are rarely people who have experience of building their own substantial wealth and passive income.

Even worse, many of them buy into the system encouraged by banks and credit companies—which is based on encouraging you to borrow large amounts of money and to keep paying interest for a very long time.

And of course, they typically have the priority of selling you financial products that make them money and build in high profits for the companies that sell them.

The real key to wealth is taking advice from people who have experience of building wealth.

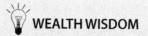

WEALTH WISDOM

If you want to be wealthy, take advice from people who have experience of building wealth.

3

SIX INSIDER SECRETS OF BECOMING DEBT-FREE AND WEALTHY

WEALTH WORKOUT 8: YOUR WEALTH MINDSET

What beliefs do you have about money that may be holding you back?

_____

_____

_____

When have you made financial decisions under the influence of emotions—and what was the result?

_____

_____

_____

How would you describe your personality in relation to money?

_____

_____

_____

Who do you take advice from on financial matters and what experience do they have of making wealth that qualifies them to advise you?

_____

_____

_____

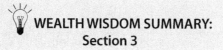

WEALTH WISDOM SUMMARY:
Section 3

- The average person in the UK will earn more than £1,200,000 over their working life, but most let it slip through their fingers.

- "Wealth accumulators" live as if they earn half of what they really do but they end up rich and can enjoy anything they like. "Consumers" behave as if they earn twice as much but they end up poor and working in their retirement years.

- The real cost of something you buy is not only what you pay for it but what you give up in the future by having spent that money rather than invested it.

- The banking system is based on lending the same money many times. When banks and credit companies lend more to you, they can lend more to others and make higher profit. That is why they want you to borrow more. However, there is a way for you to copy that approach and build your own wealth faster.

- Compound interest is where your interest earns interest. Where you make this work in your favour—through your investments—you can turn relatively small amounts into large amounts faster than you'd believe possible. If it is working against you—through your debts—small amounts quickly become very large.

- Banks borrow money from each other at relatively low rates and then lend it to you in the form of credit card debt at very high rates. They may well be making more than 1,000% profit on the money you owe them on your credit cards.

- Inflation is back and it is eating away at the value of any savings you have. There are now more things to buy, they cost more and your money buys you less every day.

3

SIX INSIDER SECRETS OF BECOMING DEBT-FREE AND WEALTHY

WEALTH WISDOM SUMMARY:
Section 3-continued

- The cost of the traditional system of providing retirement pensions is becoming unsustainable as fewer people are in the workforce and people are living longer.

- Money problems are the single biggest cause of relationship problems and can be a major cause of stress and health problems. Solving money worries can therefore improve your health and your relationships.

- Wealth-building assets increase in value or generate income. Liabilities reduce in value or cost you money.

- Good debt is used to buy something that generates income or increases in value. Bad debt buys something that reduces in value or costs you money.

- Every day we face an alliance of manufacturers, retailers and credit providers who need our money and will do everything possible to make us part with it. We need to resist this manipulation.

- Before buying or selling something, wait at least a week before doing anything. If it's a big decision, ask advice from at least one expert.

- Never buy something based on what other people own. You never know their true financial situation and they may be running into serious problems. Buy based on what you want, need and can afford.

- Think very carefully about your reasons for buying something. If you think it will make you feel better or make others like you more, find another reason.

- Improving your financial knowledge through education is one of the most important investments you can make in your future wealth.

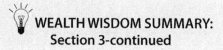

WEALTH WISDOM SUMMARY:
Section 3-continued

- The attitudes and habits we develop about money in our early days can affect us for the rest of our lives. Often it requires a conscious effort to change the way you think and behave.

- Your wealth thermostat is an unconscious control that can stop you growing your income above a certain level or make you spend too much. You may need to adjust it if you want to be wealthy.

- Get to know what type of financial personality you are so that you know how best to build your wealth strategy.

- If you want to be wealthy, take advice from people who have experience of building wealth.

3

SIX INSIDER SECRETS OF BECOMING DEBT-FREE AND WEALTHY

4

Six Essential Habits to Eliminate Debt and Become Wealthy Fast

4

SIX ESSENTIAL HABITS TO ELIMINATE DEBT AND BECOME WEALTHY FAST

AS WITH ANY MAJOR breakthroughs in life, the move from debt to wealth is not going to happen without taking action.

If you want to improve your golf swing, you are going to have to take a few lessons from an expert and get in some practice too. If you want to lose some weight, you have to change some behaviours—eating differently and doing some exercise.

The road from debt to wealth is no different.

Having good information and thinking in the right way is not going to change anything. You need to start behaving differently. You need to make a few changes in your life and then make these new behaviours the way you live from now on.

Your situation won't be totally transformed overnight but you might be surprised at how quickly you will start to see results. The first few small steps are not only rewarding, they also make a huge difference.

In this chapter, we look at the six key changes you need to make in the way you run your financial life if you want to move quickly from debt to wealth. The six essential habits are as follows:

1. Set financial goals and measure current net worth.
2. Switch your spending to cash only.
3. Stop thinking monthly and set a budget.
4. Speed up debt repayment.
5. Spend your money more wisely.
6. Start building for the future.

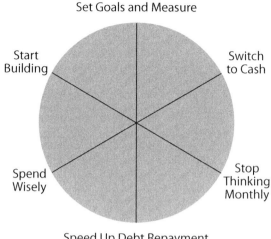

In this chapter, I'll take you through each of these habits.

This takes us through the five most important steps of the process from debt to wealth.

1. Acceptance of need to change.
2. Assessment of your current financial situation.
3. Action to change your financial situation.
4. Acceleration of debt repayment to financial freedom.
5. Accumulation of real wealth.

In the remaining chapters, we will go into the final step—accumulation of real wealth and generation of passive income—in much more detail.

WEALTH HABIT 1:
SET FINANCIAL GOALS AND MEASURE CURRENT NET WORTH

When you set out on any journey in life, you need to know two important facts—where you are now and where you want to get to. Without these two key factors, you can't make a plan for getting from one to the other.

Present Clarity

The biggest wealth challenge for many people is that they don't actually know where they stand.

Sure, they have an idea of what's in their bank account and how much they owe on their credit cards. But they can't really put their finger on the exact details. So the first step to improving your wealth is being able to measure it.

As we discussed already, one of the best measures of wealth is net worth. So, one of the first steps we will take is going through an exercise to help you work out your actual net worth so that you can keep track of it.

This step is the start of going through all your financial information so that you can get a true picture of where you are right now and get ready to take the necessary action needed to change it.

So now it is time to gather and collate all your financial information in one place.

If you've never done this process before and you don't keep very good financial records, you may find this a bit painful. But it will be a real eye-opener for you. You will need to collect all your financial information from the past twelve months such as:

- Bank statements
- Credit card bills
- Mortgage and loan statements
- Investment statements

At this stage, the process is all about getting an accurate picture of where you are. This measures your net worth—the current size of your Wealth Wheel.

In the rest of the book, we'll focus on making your wheel much bigger.

WEALTH WORKOUT 9: NET WORTH

Start by listing out all your assets—irrespective of whether they have loans attached to them.

You need to list everything of significance you own. Start by listing the highest value first and then list each item in order thereafter.

Add the numbers for assets to the second column and liabilities to the third.

When you categorize your assets and measure your net worth, it's a good idea to split your assets into wealth-building assets and other assets.

A wealth-building asset is something you own that pays you an income or that grows in value with the intention that you can sell it and capture the value.

Clear examples of wealth-building assets would be shares, art or investment property. Other assets would be the current market value of your car as this reduces in value. We count your main home under "other assets" even although it increases in value as you cannot generally realize its value while living in it.

Fill in the chart below, adding your own assets and liabilities as appropriate.

Spreadsheet 1: Net Worth

	Assets (£)	Liabilities (£)
Wealth Building Assets		
Stocks and shares		
Savings accounts		
Cash		
Other Assets		
Home		
Car		
Liabilities		
Mortgage		
Credit card balances		
Other loans		
Other liabilities		
	Total Assets	**Total Liabilities**
Total Assets LESS Total Liabilities **= NET WORTH**		

Future Vision

Now that you have worked out where you are, I want you to spend a bit of time thinking about the future.

Have you ever stopped to consider what you really want to do in your life? What would you do if money and time were no object?

You probably had dreams you abandoned earlier in your life as debt began to mount up and life seemed to be all about reaching the end of the month.

When you start turning your debt into wealth, you will be able to realise these old dreams—it's time to start believing in them again.

If you follow the system I outline in this book, they won't stay dreams for very long—they will soon become reality. Think about how you would spend your ideal day if you had no debt and you could live without working.

- How would you spend your time?
- Who would you spend time with?
- Where would you live?
- What time would you get up/go to bed?
- What would the typical day in your life look like?

This may seem a bit of a distraction at this stage but here's why it's important. It's not unusual for people who have debt problems to be spending a large amount of their time worried about debt.

The problem with that is that you get the results in your life that your mind focuses on. So if you focus on debt, you tend to get more.

> **MASTER YOUR MINDSET**
>
> You get the outcome you focus on—so it's important to focus on the outcome you want.

In the book *Psycho-Cybernetics*, Dr Maxwell Maltz explains the importance of the "mental movies" that we run in our minds every day in determining the outcomes we get in our life.

He says that if we are constantly thinking about certain outcomes they are more likely to happen. He talks about the "Theatre of the Mind" as being a place where you can run your own positive mental movies to help create the outcome you want.

You Get What You Focus On

A famous example of this is a study where three similar groups of students were asked to take part in a test looking at the best way to improve results in basketball free throws.

- One group practiced every day for twenty days.
- The second engaged in no sort of practice.
- The third group spent twenty minutes a day imagining they were throwing the ball at the goal.

At the end of twenty days the first group had shown 24% improvement, while the second showed no improvement at all. But, remarkably the third group that only imagined practicing showed a 23% improvement—virtually the same as the group that practiced for real. This shows the immense power of visualization.

If you want to change your financial situation, it makes sense to visualize success by running mental movies of what it will be like living your debt-free, financially secure life.

Running these images regularly over in your mind will help reprogram yourself.

Of course, I'm not saying to live in a dream world and forget the realities. The most important thing here is taking immediate action and the steps you are going to go through now will put that action in place.

But we are creatures of habit and, as such, we tend to move towards what is most dominant in our thoughts so you need to take control of these thoughts and start focusing on where you want to go rather than what you want to get away from.

In other words, I want you to get out of the tunnel by focusing on the bright light at the end of it rather than on the darkness behind you.

Reaching Your Destination

The process of wealth creation is like going on a journey. You need to identify your desired destination and then you need to develop a route map for getting there. Most importantly the faster the mode of transport you have and the clearer directions you have, the quicker the journey.

You can walk, run, cycle, drive, take a train, boat or plane. Each one can get you to your destination but one will be much quicker than the others. It is not just the journey but the speed in which you want to get there that will determine the best mode of transport.

To help you reach your desired destination, the next Wealth Workout is about creating a clear picture of the future you want.

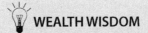

WEALTH WISDOM

Creating a clear picture of what your desired destination—financial freedom—looks like will help you get there.

WEALTH WORKOUT 10: FUTURE GOALS

Take some time to dream about the future when you have achieved financial freedom. By beginning to develop your plans, you can shape the future you want.

Cut out photos of things you see as part of your ideal lifestyle— have them somewhere you see them regularly such as on your desk, in your bathroom or in your car.

In time, you will want to make these goals very specific but starting with a big picture and making it visual gives you a clear picture of where you are heading.

WEALTH HABIT 2:
SWITCH YOUR SPENDING TO CASH ONLY

You've probably heard the saying that "Insanity is doing same thing over and over and expecting different results."

Bear that in mind every time you use your credit card. How easy do you think it will be to get out of debt if you keep adding more?

If you wanted to give up smoking, you wouldn't walk around with a packet of cigarettes in your pocket. You have to apply the same approach to debt.

You may also have heard the saying "A journey of a thousand miles begins with a single step."

Probably the single biggest step you can take in turning your debt into wealth is to get rid of your credit cards.

This is not just a temporary step. This is a new way of life.

You have to get used to only spending money that you already have. That means you have to buy everything with cash. No more borrowing and no more credit cards.

You can't get out of debt if you still have credit cards in your wallet.

The fact is you may not find this one easy if you have got used to having credit cards. For many people this means the emotionally challenging task of actually cancelling and getting rid of credit cards.

Like any addict you are probably saying you can't do that because you need them. You feel you can't live without them.

The process of giving up is not always easy, and people often ask if they can give up slowly or if there are any "patches" they can use to ease them off gently.

Well, there is one small concession allowed to ease the transition. I will let you keep just one card. It is only for emergencies and there is a very strict condition attached to it, which I will explain later.

> **MASTER YOUR MINDSET**
>
> Wealthy people associate with other positive, successful people.

So you may keep one no-annual-fee card as an emergency backup in case something goes wrong and you need urgent access to funds. Put it in a safe place and remember that it is strictly for emergencies only.

There is one good tip I give to make sure you don't get tempted to use it. Put it in an old soup can in the freezer. Then you need to let it thaw out before you use it.

By the time it thaws out, you may even decide that it wasn't really an emergency and you may even change your mind about spending the money.

Joining the Cash Economy

If you've been kidding yourself for years that your credit limit is your own money, this is a major life change. You have to remember it was *never* your money—it is somebody else's. Switching to cash is an essential step if you want to get out of debt and create real wealth.

Once you have got rid of credit cards, your only option is paying cash. That way, you have to accept that, if you can't come up with the cash, you can't afford it right now.

Of course that doesn't mean going around with a suitcase full of notes. You can use a debit card to make transactions easier. Cheques are fine too although they are becoming much less common as a way of transferring money.

But, in general, get into the habit of taking the cash out of the machine and handing it over; it connects you more to the money.

Connecting the Cost to Your Work

Another great way of connecting more directly with the true cost of something is to calculate how many hours you have to work for anything that you buy.

When you do this, you might find yourself deciding that you don't actually need it that much after all.

If something costs £150 and you earn £10 an hour, you have to work fifteen hours to buy that item. That means you need to work for more than two days, taking tax into account, just to buy that one item.

It is much more painful when you look at it like that.

If you do that with everything you buy, you will find you automatically start to spend less.

Some people have so much debt that credit cards are the only way to buy more stuff. You have to accept that if you don't have cash, you can't buy.

An added benefit of buying with cash is that you can most often negotiate a much better price so you can get much more for your money.

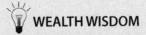

WEALTH WISDOM

Switching from credit card to cash is a vital step in increasing your connection with money and stopping new debts.

Dealing with Arrears and Other Problems

As part of the process of sorting out your cards, you should cancel any cards where you don't currently have an outstanding balance. If you have an outstanding balance, keep making the minimum payment. We'll look at how you to clear the balance completely shortly.

If you have any cards or accounts where you are behind on payments, you need to contact the provider and explain your situation. They may be able to offer you special terms to allow you to get back on track. If you have several accounts where you are behind—or you are more than a couple of months behind—you should get specialist advice on how to resolve the problem.

In the UK, one of the best options is to contact your local Citizens Advice Bureau for their help. One of the options available is that you can reach an agreement with them that will allow you to freeze all interest payments and possibly even make arrangements to settle your outstanding debts for much less than the amount due.

However, these steps can have a major impact on your credit record that you may wish to avoid. In extreme cases, you may even end up discussing bankruptcy. There are more options you can discuss that may help you get out of your current situation quicker but it makes sense to get expert advice before making any decisions.

There are many helplines and advice services that offer free debt counselling, so be careful about services that charge fees for providing this service. If you find the right help, you may be willing to pay for it, but take time to check out the other options as well.

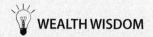 **WEALTH WISDOM**

Take appropriate advice if you have significant arrears on loans or credit cards but check out free services before agreeing to pay.

WEALTH WORKOUT 11: CUT UP YOUR CREDIT CARDS

Gather up all your credit cards and store cards and cut them up one by one. Where you have no outstanding balance, contact the providers and cancel your account.

Where you have an outstanding balance, keep paying the minimum payment for now.

Where you have arrears problems, contact the provider to discuss your situation and seek professional advice, e.g. from the Citizens Advice Bureau.

4

SIX ESSENTIAL HABITS TO ELIMINATE DEBT AND BECOME WEALTHY FAST

WEALTH HABIT 3:
STOP THINKING MONTHLY AND SET A BUDGET

You may have heard the expression that the "money ran out before the month" to cover the situation of people who can't quite make ends meet.

That's an all too common problem today. But it also reflects the big problem that too many people think only about the end of the month and not about their long-term futures.

The harsh reality is that many people spend more time arranging a weekend break than they do their long-term financial futures.

Or they might spend a whole evening doing some research to save money on their car insurance—and there is nothing wrong with that—but they spend no time at all on thinking about their long term financial future.

> **MASTER YOUR MINDSET**
>
> Poor people work for money. Wealthy people have their money working for them.

One way this becomes a problem is that they look at debts in terms of the monthly payment: "It's only £50 a month so I can easily afford this."

Then along comes the end of the month and all of your income is promised away to creditors. You don't have any income left so you need more credit. When you think monthly, you transfer your wealth to retailers, manufacturers, and credit card companies. You have to give up thinking monthly and start thinking *lifetime cost*.

Just take a look back at some of the numbers we talked about in Insider Wealth Secret #1.

Here are some of them:

- Daily takeaway coffee at £2 a day = £88,000 over thirty-five years.
- Daily sandwiches at £5 a day = £220,000 over thirty-five years.
- Regular eating out at £90 a week = £750,000 over thirty-five years.

If you budgeted more carefully and took a longer term view, you could make these numbers significantly lower.

When you take a long term view, you also realise that delaying paying debts is costing you more money.

The key to getting away from monthly thinking is to make a plan for your finances. To do this, you need to get a very clear picture of where your money is coming from and where it is going.

This means you need to dig into all these statements you gathered for the net worth exercise and really look very closely at the numbers.

In this section, we will work out a detailed budget so that you can keep control of your finances.

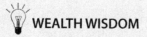 **WEALTH WISDOM**

A clear budget helps you keep control of your money and take a longer term view so that you think beyond the end of the month.

WEALTH WORKOUT 12: YOUR BUDGET

Spending time on planning your future wealth is one of the best investments you can make.

Part of this process is creating a budget for your expenditure so that you make sure the income you receive is spent well to ensure you meet your objectives.

Your budget will include the following four components:

1. Your monthly income
2. Your monthly expenditure
3. Your cash expenditure
4. Your outstanding debts and monthly repayment

1. Monthly Income

The first step in the process is to identify your monthly income.

If your monthly income is predictable this should be fairly easy. If it is variable, you will have to look back over the whole year and put in a monthly average. Make sure you include a monthly average for any occasional income.

Spreadsheet 2: Monthly Income

Monthly Income	(£)
Employment Income	
Allowance for bonuses	
Investment income (not reinvested)	
Social security benefits	
Other income	
Total Monthly Income	

2. Monthly Expenditure

In order to take control of your wealth flow, you need to get on top of where the money that comes into your life is then flowing out of it again.

That means keeping track of your expenditure.

To do this properly, you need to get into as much detail as possible.

We are going to look at a typical month but there are obviously some costs that vary a bit from month to month. So you need to look back over the whole year and put in a monthly average for quarterly or annual costs.

If you have put expenses on your credit card, list out what they are—at least in categories—rather than just putting "credit card."

Many costs will vary so you may need to include an average in each month.

This list will serve as the basis for your monthly budget.

Later, we will be looking at how you can use it as a way to reduce your expenditure.

Spreadsheet 3: Monthly Expenditure

Expenditure	(£)
Mortgage or rent	
Credit cards repayments	
Other loan repayments	
Electricity / Gas	
Phone / TV / Internet	
Insurance	
Car Costs	
Groceries	
Pension contributions	
Clothing	
Entertainment	
Total Expenditure	

3. Your Cash Outlays

As you look at your bank statements, you'll probably identify quite large amounts each month as cash withdrawals.

In order to get a proper handle on where your money is going, you need to identify where the cash goes.

So, for a week or two, you need to keep a note of every penny you spend in cash. Identify some categories such as entertainment, gifts, travel, and coffees to help you keep track.

Spreadsheet 4: Cash Outlays

Cash Outlays	(£)	Expenditure Category
Newspapers and magazines		
Lunch		
Coffees		
Drinks		
Entertainment		
Snacks		
Clothes		
Total Cash Expenditure		

4. Monthly Debt Repayment

Next step is to go into more detail with your outstanding debts. List each debt showing the amount outstanding and the current minimum monthly repayment.

Spreadsheet 5: Debt Repayment

Debt Type	Balance Outstanding (£)	Minimum Monthly Payment (£)

SIX ESSENTIAL HABITS TO ELIMINATE DEBT AND BECOME WEALTHY FAST

4

SIX ESSENTIAL HABITS TO ELIMINATE DEBT AND BECOME WEALTHY FAST

WEALTH HABIT 4:
SPEED UP DEBT REPAYMENT

One of the worst wealth-killing habits is making only the minimum repayments each month on your outstanding debts.

The fact is, every penny in debt you don't pay today is going to cost you more tomorrow.

Once you have paid your essential bills, there should be no greater priority in your budget than paying off debt.

When you start paying down debt, you quickly have more money available as you are cutting back the amount you are paying in interest.

That doesn't mean you can't have some spare cash for fun in your life. You just need to understand how much it costs you to hang on to debt longer than necessary.

Here's an example of the difference it makes. Brian has a balance of £1,200 on his credit card. The table on the next page shows how long it will take him to repay the debt if he pays only the minimum each month—which is what many people do.

The table also shows how paying a bit more each month would help him repay the debt faster—and save a lot of money.

Amount paid	Length of time to repay	Total interest payable (19.9% APR)	Total amount payable (£)
Minimum (2.5% of outstanding balance—starting at £30 the first month)	22 years 3 months	£1,955	£3,155
£50 per month	2 years 7 months	£350	£1,550
£100 per month	1 year 2 months	£200	£1,400

While he might think he is "saving" money each month by only making the minimum repayment, it's actually costing him a fortune.

By only paying the minimum, Brian will end up paying more than DOUBLE the amount he would have paid by repaying a bit extra each month.

You can see how paying off your debts slowly is costing you a fortune.

That's why it's so important to speed up the process, even if that seems a challenge right now.

This principle doesn't only apply to your credit cards—it's something you should take into account with every loan, even your mortgage.

There is a widespread belief that it's a good idea to keep your monthly mortgage payment as low as possible and to keep making payments for most of your working life—or even beyond.

This is a major wealth killer.

4

If you get into the habit of paying more than the minimum each month, you will not only reduce your debt faster, you will also develop a habit that will help you quickly increase your wealth.

Over time, the aim is to redirect the flow of money in your life so that it goes to building your future wealth instead of to credit companies.

You need to start by eliminating the debt as quickly as possible.

The Debt Destroyer Process

When you are faced with a huge debt and only have a small amount available each month to make the payments, the problem can seem impossible to overcome.

That's why you need a disciplined approach to make the payments in the best way possible.

You'll be amazed how quickly you get results, but you have to change the way you use money.

The Debt Destroyer Process is the mechanism I use to help people pay off their debts as quickly as possible.

The Debt Destroyer Process is an accelerated plan for paying off your debts and can allow you to be totally debt-free in just a few years even just using your current income.

In other words, the income that got you into debt can also get you out of it!

Here is how it works:

- You pay the minimum monthly payment on all your debts.

- You allocate an additional amount of money each month to be used for *one* accelerated debt repayment. I call this the Debt Destroyer Payment. I suggest you start off by making this 10% of your net monthly income. (That may seem a lot if you are struggling to make payments right now but in the next section, I'll show you that it's probably easier to find spare cash than you think.)

- You use this Debt Destroyer Payment to reduce your debts by focusing it on *one* debt at a time. I usually advise people to start by paying off the smallest debt first. This gets the fastest positive result and provides a good sense of making progress.

- Once that debt is repaid, you then take your Debt Destroyer Payment *plus* the minimum payment that you had been paying on the first debt, and apply them both to the next debt in line.

This is a vital part of the process.

It is easy to feel a sense of relief when one debt is paid off. We can easily be tempted to take that money and spend it on something else or even take on more debt. It's normal human nature to try and fill a void like this.

For this process to work, it is crucial to maintain the discipline and focus the money that has been freed up into the Debt Destroyer Process.

I'm not saying that you should never enjoy a little reward once in a while. But you must get into the habit of focusing as much money as possible on paying down your debt.

Then you will be ready to start enjoying your financial freedom.

- When all your debts are repaid, your Debt Destroyer Payment will have grown into quite a substantial monthly sum that you can then use to invest for your future.

Can you see that the Debt Destroyer Payment acts just like that snowball rolling downhill?

Your payment may be small at first but when it starts rolling, as you repay your debts, it builds momentum.

When it reaches its destination it can be huge.

That's how we manage to help people pay off their debts so quickly.

Let's look at an example to show how this works.

Suzy has various debts totalling £125,000. The following table lists them in order with the smallest debt at the top and the largest at the bottom:

Debt Type	Balance Outstanding	Rate of Interest APR%	Monthly Payment	Repayment Term
Store card	£3,000	23.7%	£75	5 years 7 months
MasterCard	£4,000	15.9%	£100	4 years 5 months
Visa	£6,000	19.9%	£150	5 years 1 month
Car loan	£12,000	9%	£249	5 years
Mortgage	£100,000	4.5%	£556	25 years
TOTALS	**£125,000**		**£1,130**	

Here are some important points to note about these numbers:

- The rate of interest is the current Annual Percentage Rate (APR) for each debt.

- The monthly payment is the minimum allowed by the lender. (For mortgages, you can arrange to have interest-only payments for a short while until all other debts have been cleared—this will release an even larger amount towards the Debt Destroyer Payment.)

- The repayment term is how long it would take to clear the full debt making the monthly payment shown.

If Suzy goes on like this, she will still be in debt in twenty-five years' time—even without adding more in the future.

So, let's have a look at how much faster she can get out of debt by following the Debt Destroyer Process.

She has net monthly income of £2,000 a month, so, in addition to her monthly minimum payments, **she sets an initial Debt Destroyer Payment of 10% of her income, or** £200 a month.

She pays the minimum monthly amount on all her debts and applies that extra payment of £200 to the smallest debt, which is her store card. This is how her monthly repayments look next month...

Debt Type	Balance Outstanding	Rate of Interest APR%	Monthly Payment	Repayment Term
Store card	£3,000	23.7%	£75 + £ 200 = £275 Debt Destroyer Payment	12 months
MasterCard	£4,000	15.9%	£100	4 years 5 months
Visa	£6,000	19.9%	£150	5 years 1 month
Car loan	£12,000	9%	£249	5 years
Mortgage	£100,000	4.5%	£556	25 years
TOTALS	**£125,000**		**£1,330**	**25 years**

As a result of this process, she will pay her store card off in twelve months instead of nearly six years.

When the store card is fully repaid, she then switches her Debt Destroyer Payment of £200 a month *plus* the £75 she was previously paying on the store card to the next debt in line, which is the MasterCard.

Added to her existing monthly repayment on that card, she now has a new Debt Destroyer Payment of £375.

Debt Type	Balance Outstanding	Rate of Interest APR%	Monthly Payment	Repayment Term
MasterCard	£4,000	15.9%	£100 + £275 = £375 Debt Destroyer Payment	1 year 9 months
Visa	£6,000	19.9%	£150	5 years 1 month
Car loan	£12,000	9%	£249	5 years
Mortgage	£100,000	4.5%	£556	25 years
TOTALS	**£122,000**		**£1,330**	**25 years**

By applying those additional payments to the MasterCard, she will pay it off in one year and nine months instead of taking more than four years.

When the MasterCard is repaid, she continues that process by moving on to the next debt in her list—the Visa. She adds the £375 freed up to the £150 minimum payment she is already making. This gives her a new Debt Destroyer Payment of £525.

Debt Type	Balance Outstanding	Rate of Interest APR%	Monthly Payment	Repayment Term
Visa	£6,000	19.9%	£150 + £375 = £525 Debt Destroyer Payment	2 years 5 months
Car loan	£12,000	9%	£249	5 years
Mortgage	£100,000	4.5%	£556	25 years
TOTALS	**£118,000**		**1,330**	**25 years**

SIX ESSENTIAL HABITS TO ELIMINATE DEBT AND BECOME WEALTHY FAST

4

That extra payment enables her to clear the Visa bill in just over two years and she can now apply the extra payment to her car loan...

Debt Type	Balance Outstanding	Rate of Interest APR%	Monthly Payment	Repayment Term
Car loan	£12,000	9%	£249 + £525 = £774 Debt Destroyer Payment	3 years 3 months
Mortgage	£100,000	4.5%	£556	25 years
TOTALS	**£112,000**		**£1,330**	**25 years**

So, when she has followed this process through with all her non-mortgage debts, she has built up a Debt Destroyer Payment of £774 a month.

This means she will have paid off *all* her non-mortgage debts in just over three years instead of taking more than five years making just the minimum monthly repayments.

That's already saving her a great deal of money but look at what happens when she moves to the next stage. Now she adds the £774 to the mortgage payment and starts paying a total of £1,330 each month towards her mortgage:

Debt Type	Balance Outstanding	Rate of Interest APR%	Monthly Payment	Repayment Term
Mortgage	£100,000	4.5%	£556 + £774 = £1,330 Debt Destroyer Payment	10 years
TOTALS	**£100,000**		**£1,330**	**10 years**

That means she will pay off all her cards _and_ her mortgage in just ten years.

So, instead of being burdened with debt for twenty-five years, following the Debt Destroyer Process means Suzy will be totally debt-free in only ten years.

Suzy saves not only time but money. The table on the next page shows how much she has saved by following the Debt Destroyer Process, rather than making unnecessary interest payment by paying the minimum only.

Debt Type	Making Minimum Payments Only		Following Debt Destroyer System	
	Repayment Term	Total Payments	Repayment Term	Total Payments
Store card	5 years 7 months	£5,025	12 months	£3,300
MasterCard	4 years 5 months	£5,300	1 year 9 months	£4,416
Visa	5 years 1 month	£9,150	2 years 7 months	£8,012
Car loan	5 years	£14,940	3 years 3 months	£13,914
Mortgage	25 years	£166,800	10 years	£129,407
TOTALS	**25 years**	**£201,215**	**10 years**	**£159,049**

She has saved a total of £42,166 in interest payments that she will not now have to make.

However, not only has she avoided wasting a large sum on interest payments, she has built up the habit of putting aside £1,330 every month.

This is where she can stop thinking about repaying debt and start focusing on building wealth.

By using that money every month to turn the wealth flow towards her, she can start investing to achieve financial freedom.

Isn't that a much better way to use her hard-earned cash rather than wasting it by giving it away in interest payments to banks and credit card companies?

And, just imagine how much faster she could reach that stage if she were able to make a few savings and allocate even more of her money each month to destroying debt!

Next I'll show you step-by-step how you can decide what you need to do to achieve the same objective.

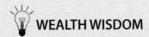 **WEALTH WISDOM**

Paying off debts as fast as you can means you pay less in interest and free up your cash sooner for something better.

WEALTH WORKOUT 13: YOUR DEBT DESTROYER PAYMENT

Now it is time to decide how much you can allocate each month as your Debt Destroyer Payment.

This is the extra amount you need to pay each month on top of your current minimum payments to reduce your debt faster.

I suggest you start with 10% of your net income—more if possible. For example, if your net income is £2,000, you will allocate £200 as your monthly Debt Destroyer Payment.

You will need to add this in to your monthly expenditure budget that you created in spreadsheet 3.

Write your initial monthly Debt Destroyer Payment here (at least 10% of your net income):

Be prepared to come back and review it after the next chapter, where we focus on how you can cut your expenditure and free up even more cash to destroy debt.

WEALTH WORKOUT 14: YOUR DEBT DESTROYER PAYMENT— ORDER OF PRIORITY

To enable you to get started using the Debt Destroyer Process, you need to decide which debt to focus on first.

This is one of the most important steps in the process of turning your debt into wealth. When you start seeing how much more quickly you will get out of debt using this process, it will be inspiring and motivational.

We'll work through the elements step by step.

Step 1: List Out Debts

Start by taking the debts and minimum monthly payments you worked out in spreadsheet 5 and list them in order with the smallest debt at the top and the largest at the bottom. Check with the lenders to make sure you are making the minimum monthly payment on each debt.

Debt Type	Balance Outstanding	Minimum Monthly Payment
Mortgage		
TOTALS		

Step 2: Calculate Exact Repayment Term

The next step is to work out how long it will take you to repay each debt by just paying the minimum monthly amount.

You will need to contact each of the credit/loan providers on your list and ask them how long it will take to repay the debt if you only make the minimum monthly payment.

To get an idea of the total amount payable, multiply the minimum monthly payment by the repayment term remaining. This will not give you the exact term but will give you a good indication.

Example

The table below shows the numbers for Suzy from the example in the previous section.

Debt Type	Balance Outstanding	Monthly Payment	Repayment Term Remaining	Total Payable
Store card	£3,000	£75	5 years 7 months	£5,025
MasterCard	£4,000	£100	4 years 5 months	£5,300
Visa	£6,000	£150	5 years 1 month	£9,150
Car loan	£12,000	£249	5 years	£14,940
Mortgage	£100,000	£556	25 years	£166,800
TOTALS	**£125,000**	**£1,130**		**£201,215**

Now use the table below to fill in your own numbers.

Debt Type	Balance Outstanding	Monthly Payment	Repayment Term Remaining	Total Payable
Mortgage				
TOTALS				

4

SIX ESSENTIAL HABITS TO ELIMINATE DEBT AND BECOME WEALTHY FAST

Step 3: Adding the Debt Destroyer Payments

Next, we are going to work out how you can use the Debt Destroyer Payment to repay the loan faster.

- Start by using the same table as Step 1 with all the balances and monthly payments filled in with the smallest debt at the top and largest at the bottom.

- Then write in the initial Debt Destroyer Payment you decided in Wealth Workout 13 into the shaded box in the following table. It should be at least 10% of your net monthly income. (In the example, it is £200.)

- Next add the initial Debt Destroyer Payment to the first monthly debt payment which should be in the row below. This gives you the new Debt Destroyer Payment. (In the example, it is £200 + £75 = £275.)

- Keep working down the list adding the Debt Destroyer Payment to the monthly payment below it. For example, the next one is £275 + £100 = £375. This payment starts after the previous debt has been fully repaid. The process then continues with the next Debt Destroyer Payment beginning after this debt has been repaid.

Debt Type	Balance Outstanding	Minimum Monthly Payment	Debt Destroyer Payment
			£200
Store card	£3,000	£75	£275
MasterCard	£4,000	£100	£375
Visa	£6,000	£150	£525
Car loan	£12,000	£249	£774
Mortgage	£100,000	£556	£1330

Follow the same process to work out your own numbers, starting by adding your chosen Debt Destroyer Payment from Wealth Workout 13 in the shaded box.

Debt Type	Balance Outstanding	Minimum Monthly Payment	Debt Destroyer Payment
			(At least 10% of net income)
Mortgage			

Step 4: Work Out Change in New Repayment Term

The next step is to work out how much faster your debts will be repaid using the Debt Destroyer Process.

You can work this out by dividing the Balance Outstanding by the Debt Destroyer Payment.

In the example, the first debt—the store card—would be £3,000 divided by £275, which is eleven months. We follow the same process for each debt.

Debt Type	Balance Outstanding	Minimum Monthly Payment	Debt Destroyer Payment	Time to Repay Debt Balance / Debt Destroyer
			£200	
Store card	£3,000	£75	£275	11 months
MasterCard	£4,000	£100	£375	11 months
Visa	£6,000	£150	£525	11 months
Car loan	£12,000	£249	£774	16 months
Mortgage	£100,000	£556	£1330	75 months
TOTAL TERM	–	–	–	124 months (10 years 4 months)

You may notice that the estimated repayment terms are slightly different from those that appeared in this example in the previous section. That is because this method gives you an approximate answer which is a useful indication. The previous example was calculated more precisely.

In addition, these monthly periods are cumulative, which means the second period of eleven months begins after the first period is complete and so on.

When you have completed the final column for each debt, add together the timings for all the debts. In the example above, the total is just over ten years.

Remember, these are approximate numbers. The actual repayment terms will be slightly shorter because your balances will be reducing as you continue to make monthly repayments on the other debts.

What's important is to see the difference between these numbers and the ones we worked out at Step 2.

In Suzy's example, the first debt is repaid in less than a year instead of more than five years).

All the debts are repaid in just over ten years instead of twenty-five years.

So now work out your own numbers by following the same process of dividing the Balance Outstanding by the Debt Destroyer Payment.

Debt Type	Balance Outstanding	Minimum Monthly Payment	Debt Destroyer Payment	Time to Repay Debt Balance / Debt Destroyer
Mortgage				
TOTAL TERM				

It is very important to bear in mind that the repayment terms are approximate.

However this exercise should give you a clear idea of how much faster you can get out of debt by following the Debt Destroyer Process. Hopefully you can also see that increasing the Debt Destroyer Payment will make this work even faster. So, in the next section, I'm going to talk about steps you can take to free up more money for debt repayment.

4

SIX ESSENTIAL HABITS TO ELIMINATE DEBT AND BECOME WEALTHY FAST

WEALTH HABIT 5:
SPEND YOUR MONEY MORE WISELY

Most people who are in debt think the solution to their problems is having more income.

The truth is that people don't have financial problems due to lack of income. The problem is poor spending habits.

They think they're not earning enough, but the reality is that if they earned more they'd just spend more.

The real secret of getting out of debt and creating wealth is to hang on to more of the money you have.

MASTER YOUR MINDSET

Wealthy people focus on opportunities. Poor people focus on obstacles.

That means reviewing your spending habits very carefully.

You have to put a pause button into your mind and decide if something you are thinking of buying is really what you want and—more importantly—need.

You also need to make sure you are getting the best value for every single penny you spend.

As long as you have debt, every pound you spend is a pound you are not using for debt repayment and therefore it is costing you more in extra interest.

When you spend £150 on a new iPod, it's not just costing you £150; it's also costing you the interest on the £150 debt that you could have paid off instead.

Change Your Spending Mindset

In order to take control of your wealth, you need to develop a "minimize spending" mindset. This allows you to allocate the maximum amount to increasing your Debt Destroyer Payment.

The key to that is minimizing what you spend on everything else. In short, it's time to annihilate waste in your spending.

You may well think you don't have any spare cash at the moment. But you'll find this process a real eye-opener and, in future, you'll always be incredibly careful about how you spend your money.

You need to develop the habit of spending your money properly. You need to start spending money only on things you really need and you need to be ruthless about this. This is one reason why switching to cash helps.

Without discipline, if your income increases, you simply end up spending more.

The good news about this process is that you'll learn to use exactly the same income that got you *into* debt to get you *out of* debt. There's no need to hope for a win on the lottery or a big promotion at work.

The harsh reality is that you have to be brutally honest with yourself and face up to the fact that you have been buying things you don't really need. Here are three of the biggest problems to look out for:

1. **Convenience**: Paying someone else to do something you could do yourself; going out to lunch, convenience foods.
2. **Indulgence**: Spending money to make yourself feel better, impulse buying.
3. **Appearance**: Keeping up with Joneses, buying things to impress other people.

You may think you've got no money to spend but you will probably be shocked at how some of these costs mount up.

In the next section, I'm going to take you through a detailed process for reviewing all your expenditure but there's a simple "mantra" I learned from Martin Lewis of MoneySavingExpert.com that you should always keep in mind before buying something.

The approach varies slightly depending on your financial situation.

If you have limited resources, ask yourself the following questions before you buy anything:

1. Do I need it?
2. Can I afford it?
3. Have I checked if it's cheaper anywhere else?

Quite simply, if the answer to any of these questions is 'No' or 'Don't Know', STOP! DON'T BUY IT!

If your resources are not so limited, and you can afford to buy the item, ask yourself the following questions:

1. Will I use it?
2. Is it worth it?
3. Have I checked if it's cheaper anywhere else?

If the answer to any of these questions is 'No' or 'Don't Know', STOP! DON'T BUY IT!

Something else you need to learn is the art of negotiation. Don't just accept the price people give you. Always be ready to ask for a better deal, especially if you are paying cash as they get the money now without having to pay any transaction fees.

All these changes may seem like overkill or may seem tiny in their own right. But, taken together, they could easily save you up to 20% of your normal monthly expenditure adding up to £200 or even more each month to your Debt Destroyer Payment.

It's all designed to give you a better lifestyle and to make you smarter in the way you use your financial resources.

Here is the harsh reality:

- Every pound you spend now is costing you one pound plus additional interest costs.

- Every pound you use to reduce your debt is one that you can later invest in your future to increase your overall wealth by up to five, ten or twenty times that original amount.

It's not just about getting out of debt; it's about going all the way to creating wealth.

The key to creating significant wealth is having significant money to invest each month and the first step to doing that is taking control of your spending.

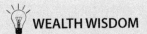

WEALTH WISDOM

Spending your money wisely leaves more cash for the things you regard as important.

The Waste Annihilator Wheel

So that you can start questioning every penny you spend, I'm going to introduce you to the Waste Annihilator Wheel.

Waste Annihilator Wheel

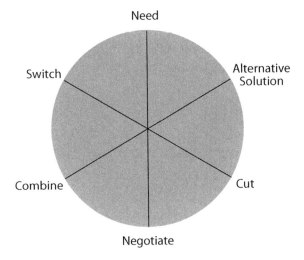

To get the best out of it, you need to ask yourself these six questions in relation to ever single penny in your budget:

1. Do I need this item? Is it absolutely essential?
2. Is there another way to meet this need—cheaper or free?
3. Can I reduce the service to cut the cost?
4. Can I negotiate a lower price with the same supplier?
5. Can I combine this service with another from the same or another provider to reduce the cost?
6. Can I switch provider for lower cost?

You have to approach this step as if you don't have any money. As you go through these steps, you may have to face some tough discussions with your partner or family, especially if you have young children. However, with children, use it as an opportunity to teach them about the real value of money.

As I mentioned before, look especially closely at the cash you spend. Keeping track of your cash spending for a few days will help you spot the patterns of where your cash goes and will help you avoid these influences.

In a moment, I'm going to show you exactly how you can start finding more money to destroy your debt and build wealth fast. You need to use the Waste Annihilator Wheel and the questions above to go through every penny you spend and make sure the expenditure is both necessary and the best possible value.

If one particular area of expenditure is causing you problems, you may have to develop a specific strategy to deal with it. For example, if you are spending a lot on eating out, you'll need to find ways to spend less on that.

Maybe you should just treat yourself once a month and use 50% vouchers to make your money stretch much further. This strategy should become a permanent part of your life—not just a one-off exercise. Once you start making these savings you will love knowing you are getting the best price on everything that you buy.

This can and should be fun and you should treat it as a game (after all, most of us enjoy playing and winning games!).

Money Saving Tips

Here are some tips on ways you can cut your costs:

General Advice

- **Negotiate:** Never accept the first deal you are offered. Always look for a better deal and be ready to walk away. Compare at least three different suppliers and pitch one against the other to get the best deal.

- **Use Coupons and Discount Brands:** Even saving 10% a month on your grocery bill using a few coupons or discount brands can add a significant amount to your Debt Destroyer Payment. Even if you spend only £100 per week, that works out to more than £500 a year saved.

- **Check Out Online Offers and Discounters**: These days there are many options for going online to get great discounts on items you normally buy and can save you up to 75% on your normal expenditure. Get into the habit of checking out the growing range of online discount services such as Groupon, which can offer many great bargains for things you were planning to buy.

- **Use Cashback and Rebates:** Most people don't bother clipping the coupons and sending off for refunds and rebates but it could easily be worth quite a bit over the year—even if you use the cashback for a special treat, why not give it a try?

- **Avoid Extended Warranties:** With most new products, if they are going to break down, they will do so in the first year and this is always covered by guarantee. Most people don't realise that the manufacturer has a duty to ensure the product is fit for use and most products should have a usable life of between three and five years. If you go directly to the manufacturer they will probably repair the product for free.

- **Shop for Necessity Not Fun**: Make sure you approach shopping as a way of buying things you need, not as a hobby. If you are bored, find a cheaper form of recreation. And certainly don't use shopping for therapy.

In the Home

- Keep your utility providers under annual review and also take steps to minimise your usage. Simple steps such as switching off lights or equipment when not in use can make a big difference. Do not keep anything on standby as that eats electricity too, **you can save between 10-20%** off your bills just by applying this strategy alone.

- For heating, adjust your clothing before you adjust the thermostat. Put on a sweater if you feel cold rather than turning up the central heating. Turning down the thermostat by just one to three degrees will make a huge difference on your gas, electric or oil bills, **saving between 10-20%.**

- Don't use TV for background noise—try the radio instead!

Car and Motoring

- Remember that the purpose of buying a car is to get you from A to B. When you see your car as an extension of your personality, you are going to spend too much on it. Despite what you might think, most wealthy people don't drive expensive, new cars.

- Never buy a brand new car—they lose 30-50% in value in the first two or three years. Instead, you should buy a car that's two or three years old sold by someone who doesn't understand this concept—you effectively get it half price or even less!

- When you do buy a car, pay cash! No financing deals allowed. When I bought my last car it was three years old with only 20,000 miles on the clock and I saved over 65% off the original purchase price. That didn't even take into account all of the upgrades the first owner paid for when it was new—these are never taken in to account when you buy or sell second hand.

- However, make sure your car is well maintained and regularly serviced. It will save you money in the long-run and will help it maintain its value when you come to sell it.

Leisure

- Do you stop at Starbucks for a latte every day because you hate the free machine in the office? Remember the numbers I shared about how much that will cost you over twenty to thirty years.

- If you pick up your lunch at the local sandwich bar instead of making it at home, have you thought about how much these few minutes saved are costing you?

- Look at cutting back on buying gifts—especially expensive ones. Cut out some of the people you buy for or reduce the amount you spend. Some very meaningful gifts can be free or very low cost. Perhaps you can give someone your time to help with something rather than buying a present.

- Holidays can be especially tricky if you have a young family; they always want to go somewhere exciting. The first question you should consider is whether you really have to go at all. Sure holidays make great family memories but not if you have to give up the home to get them. There are many ways to reduce the cost of holidays ranging from making it a long weekend rather than a week to self-catering or home swaps. Last minute deals can **save up to 75% of the original cost.** However you can only go if you can pay for it with cash, no credit card or loans.

Clothes

- First question you should ask when buying clothing has to be whether you really need it. Think about all the items you have in your wardrobe right now that you have only worn once or twice or never! When you do buy clothes, focus on the outlet stores and discount centres. Always aim to buy clothes you need from the end of season sales.

- Make sure you buy higher quality clothes with timeless styles and basic colours for maximum usage benefit. These clothes may be a little more to buy in the first instance but the way they are made and the quality is much higher. They will last a long time and will always look good.

Insurance

- Review all your insurance policies regularly and look for any overlaps in cover or unused services. Look into raising policy excesses and you may find that the savings pay for themselves very quickly. Any time you change insurance make sure the new policy is in effect before you cancel an old one.

- The purpose of life insurance is to replace the income of the income earner if they die. It is not designed to make your heirs wealthy or better their lives. It is to keep them where they would have been if you were still around.

  Life insurance is usually not a good investment vehicle so don't buy it for that purpose. You should have cover for a sum that your heirs can invest so that it is equal to your *net* annual income. For example, Family Income Benefit Term Assurance can cover you until your retirement and this is one of the cheapest types of life insurance product you can buy. This can save up to 75% of normal life insurance premiums.

Groceries and Food

- Do you usually buy ready-made dinners instead of making a low-cost meal? Adding up the cost over ten or twenty years could easily amount to £10,000-£20,000 even without factoring in what that amount would have grown to if you had invested it instead!

- The first key to cutting your grocery bill is to shop with a detailed list and to stick to it. Never shop when you are hungry and take care to avoid the temptations that are placed around the store encouraging you to buy things you don't need.

- Decline politely when offered tasters. Keep your eyes ahead when you are in the checkout area—you don't need that special offer next to the till. Behave as if you were in an area full of pickpockets—that's exactly what the store wants to do to your money so don't let them.

- Notice which shops are best for specific items and plan your shopping accordingly.

- Buying your weekly shopping online is the easiest way to restrict your spending. Firstly, most things you buy are the same each week and—as the system remembers your previous shopping—you only need to add items to your order that have run out. Also they will always tell you which product is similar or on special offer which can **save you between 20-40% on your bill.**

- When shopping, take care to avoid being tempted by all the products at eye level in the supermarket. This is the area where the most expensive products are—it is prime marketing real estate. When you look just above or below eye level, you will usually get a chance to buy a cheaper version. Items just above eye level are often between 20-30% cheaper and **those items just below eye level are 30-50% cheaper**. The beauty of shopping this way is that those products are normally made by the same manufacturer and at the same factory as the more expensive alternative; the only difference is the packaging.

- If it suits your needs, an occasional trip to Costco or other bulk retailer might help you. But you'll defeat the purpose if you end up buying things you don't need or if you buy too much of something and end up wasting it. This can easily happen especially when it comes to buying perishable goods such as food.

Money-saving Resources

There are many great resources available to help you save money either by giving you access to valuable advice and information or helping you buy below the normal cost. Here are a few of the ones I use most:

www.moneysupermarket.com
www.moneysavingexpert.com
www.groupon.com
www.gumtree.com
www.ebay.com
www.priceline.com
ww.amazon.com
www.topcashback.com
www.uswitch.com

There are many more options available in specific areas or countries and a quick Google search for "saving money on [chosen topic]" will yield even more.

WEALTH WORKOUT 15: WASTE ANNIHILATOR

For this step, we need to go back to spreadsheet 3 where we identified your monthly expenditure budget.

The purpose of this step is to go through every item using the Wealth Annihilator Wheel and questions to identify savings you can make on your spending. Then in the final column, put in the revised monthly amount.

Once you have done that go back and revise your monthly budget and your Debt Destroyer Payment.

Here is a reminder of the Wealth Annihilator questions:

- Do I need this item? Is it absolutely essential?
- Is there another way to meet this need—cheaper or free?
- Can I reduce the service to cut the cost?
- Can I negotiate a lower price with the same supplier
- Can I combine this service with another from the same or another provider to reduce the cost?
- Can I switch provider for lower cost?

Spreadsheet 6: Reducing Expenditure

Expenditure	Current Cost (£)	Possible Reduction (£)	New Cost (£)
Total Expenditure			

WEALTH HABIT 6:
START BUILDING FOR THE FUTURE

Once you have finished the Debt Destroyer process and you are totally debt-free, you are ready to begin the process of wealth building.

Establishing an Emergency Fund

Before you start building for the long-term, it's a good idea to shore up short-term security with an emergency fund. This needs to be in a liquid fund that is easily convertible back into cash.

The reality is that most people are only two months away from insolvency—if they lost their source of income, they couldn't continue to pay their expenses for more than a couple of months.

That makes you pretty vulnerable and the whole idea of debt-free living is to become *in*vulnerable.

Your goal is to be isolated from life's rollercoaster ups and downs.

If you have too much debt and suddenly you lose your job, you can easily lose your home. When you have paid off your debts, you don't have that worry. By paying off your debts, you raise the floor of your life—you can fall further and still be fine.

But unexpected events can still happen, so before tying up your money in longer term investments, you want to set aside an emergency fund that would cover six months of your normal living expenses.

174

Therefore, after you have paid off your final debt, you will need to set aside the Debt Destroyer Payment for a bit longer so that you can build up an emergency fund.

When you have your six-month emergency fund in place, it's time to start building real wealth!

The Wealth Building Process

You've used a great deal of discipline to pay off all your debts and you need to follow the same principles if you want to build serious wealth.

If you see paying off debt only as an end in itself, you will struggle to move on to wealth. To build wealth you need to retain the same principles of looking after your money that you used for debt repayment.

Why would you want to start wasting money now that you actually have some of your own? You will likely be even more motivated to make every penny work as hard as possible.

I'd therefore like to introduce you to the Asset Allocation Wheel that will help you create a disciplined system for building wealth while still giving yourself the chance to have some fun now.

The six spokes of the wheel are as follows:

1. **Living Expenses:** Essential day-to-day living costs.
2. **Short-term Investments:** Investments tied up for the next year or two.
3. **Long-term Investments:** Funds you are building for five, ten or more years ahead.
4. **Fun:** Money set aside for pleasures and luxuries.
5. **Holidays:** Money set aside for holidays during the year.
6. **Future:** This covers investment in your financial education and, if you wish, charitable donations.

The Asset Allocation Wheel

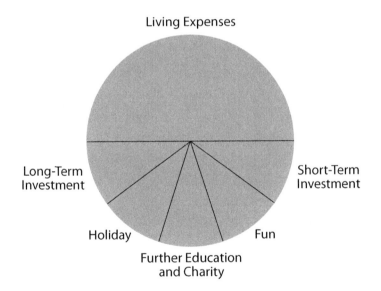

1. Living Expenses
Long-Term Investment
Short-Term Investment
Holiday
Fun
Further Education and Charity

1. Living Expenses

Once you have paid off all your debts, including your mortgage, you should be able to live on around half of your net income. Most people use more than half of their income repaying debts!

I therefore suggest you allocate up to 50% of your net income for paying normal living expenses.

2. Short-Term Investments

I recommend that you allocate around 10% of your net income for short-term investments such as bonds, Individual Savings Accounts and high-interest accounts.

These are not intended as your emergency funds so the best guidance for these investments is that there should be a strong disincentive to touch your money.

For example, you may have to give up interest if you cash them in early but you receive a higher return in exchange for this.

3. Long-Term Investments

I also recommend that you set aside 10% of your net income for longer term investment.

This is the area where you begin to build real assets. Remember an asset is something you own that pays you income or increases in value with the intention that you can sell it and capture the value.

Possible ways to build assets include:

- **Retirement Funds:** Depending on your financial situation, there may be tax benefits in making some of your investments through the vehicle of a pension plan. However, I always recommend that you make choices for the overall long-term financial benefits and not just to save some tax.

- **Shares:** Buying shares in individual companies can be profitable but can also be time-consuming especially if you want a low-stress lifestyle. You may not want to be spending your time reading the *Financial Times* or similar newspapers or magazines.

- **Unit Trusts:** This is like investing in a company that invests in other assets of many types. The advantages include diversity of investment, professional management, research and limited paperwork. When you choose funds that track market indices, you save the cost of active fund managers.

- **Property:** Investing in property can be a sound long-term choice. But you need to decide if you want to be a landlord or invest with a manager. If you do your homework well, residential and commercial property can be a real asset and create both long term wealth and passive income. You need to make mental transition that you are going in to business and not buying for yourself to live in. We cover property investment in a lot more detail in the next section.

- **Art and Antiques:** These forms of investment can be very successful provided you work with someone who has extensive experience and specialist knowledge of the field.

Choosing which of these is most appropriate depends on your own situation and preferences.

Whichever you choose, you need to make sure you have the right advisers. However, if you really want to be wealthy, never rely completely on your advisers.

Make sure you invest in your own education so that you know what you are doing and can take full advantage of the opportunities.

The Golden Goose Principle

When you invest for the future, it's important to bear in mind the Golden Goose principle. There are several variations of this traditional tale but the basic principle is that a man owned a goose that laid a golden egg every day.

He was initially quite happy with the daily golden egg but he started to get greedy and decided that there must be a huge lump of gold inside the goose. So he killed the goose in order to get to the piece of gold.

It turned out that the goose inside was just like any other goose. In his rush for some instant gratification, he deprived himself of the daily golden egg.

The moral of the tale is that if you want to keep receiving your golden egg, you must never harm the golden goose.

What that means in term of your investment is that you must never touch the capital of your investment.

In addition, if you want to maintain the full value of compound growth, you usually want to make sure that all dividends and growth are reinvested.

As long as you leave your Golden Goose intact, it will continue to generate **capital growth** and **passive income** forever. In addition, remember that the bigger your Golden Goose (your investment) gets, the bigger the eggs it lays.

4. Fun

Rather like being on a diet, you won't stick to a wealth-building plan if it does not make any provisions for you to have a treat once in a while. I therefore suggest that you allocate about 10% of your net income to your Fun Account for extra treats and expenses.

5. Holidays

In the same way as for fun, it's important that you allocate a specific amount of money to save for holidays. The exact amount will vary slightly between different people but I suggest around 10% of your net income.

6. Future

If you want to build wealth, I believe that one of your most important investments is in your own financial education.

The better your knowledge, the more money you will make. It's as simple as that. So I suggest allocating about 5% for buying books and home-study courses, attending seminars, and paying experts.

I know many people also believe that giving to charity is an important part of the wealth-building process. So I typically suggest allocating about 5% of your net income for that as well. That, of course, is entirely optional.

Allocation Percentages

The typical allocation percentages I suggest are therefore as follows.

	% of Net Income
Living Expenses	50%
Short-term Investments	10%
Long-term Investments	10%
Fun	10%
Holidays	10%
Financial Education and/or Charity	10%

The exact amounts can vary a little between individuals. For example, if you can live on less than 50% of your net income, you can allocate more funds to long-term investment.

What is most important is developing a system that you can follow in a disciplined way.

SETTING UP SPECIAL ACCOUNTS

You can operate this system just by allocating the set amounts of money in your spreadsheets, but if you can easily set up different bank accounts for each fund, that can be even more effective.

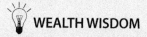

WEALTH WISDOM

Creating wealth for the future requires the same discipline and principles as paying off debts.

WEALTH WORKOUT 16: BUILDING FOR THE FUTURE

This step is only to be completed once you have completely repaid all your debts.

- **Step One:** Establish an Emergency Fund to cover all your living expenses for at least six months.
- **Step Two:** Allocate your net income on the basis set out in this chapter or adapt it slightly to suit your own preferences.

LIFE STORIES: HOW JACK AND KATE GOT OUT OF DEBT

Jack and Kate are in their mid-forties with one teenage daughter and both work full time. I began working with them when they faced serious financial problems due to having more than £80,000 of credit card debts in addition to a mortgage of more than £250,000.

With about 60% of their £3,000 net monthly income going in debt repayments, they were struggling to make ends meet and were behind on some payments. Their relationship was suffering and both were on medication for stress.

We worked out a strategy including the following:

- Remortgaging their home with a lower interest rate and more future flexibility.

- Negotiating deals on their other debts to freeze interest payments or settle on special terms.

- Applying the Debt Destroyer approach to focus maximum possible on remaining debt repayments.

- Using the Waste Annihilator to save hundreds of pounds a month from their expenditure.

This enabled them to clear the non-mortgage debts in just over four years and they are on course to clear the mortgage five years after that, making it under nine years to pay off *all* their debts.

They are already working on a wealth-building strategy that will enable them to retire earlier than they expected. This includes learning more about how they can profit from property using other people's money.

WEALTH WISDOM SUMMARY:
Section 4

- Creating a clear picture of what your desired destination—financial freedom—looks like will help you get there.

- Switching from credit card to cash is a vital step in increasing your connection with money and stopping you building up new debts.

- Take appropriate advice if you have significant arrears on loans or credit cards, but check out the free services before agreeing to pay.

- A clear budget helps you keep control of your money and take a longer term view so that you think beyond the end of the month.

- Paying off debts as fast as you can means you pay less in interest and you free up your cash sooner for something better.

- Spending your money wisely leaves more cash for the things you regard as important.

- Creating wealth for the future requires the same discipline and principles as paying off debts.

5

Six Steps to Creating Wealth and Passive Income from Property

5

WHEN I BEGAN SEARCHING for the best solution to the challenge of wealth creation some fifteen years ago, it became clear to me almost immediately that all the really wealthy people I knew, met and had read about had made most of their wealth and passive income from property and real estate.

It was a very big part of the foundation of their wealth and financial freedom.

I really wanted to be able to do the same. However I wasn't sure if it was possible for somebody like me, having at that time no background in finance and no significant money or assets of my own.

Fortunately I came across a system that taught and showed how anyone could turn real estate and property into genuine wealth, even if they had no funds or very limited funds of their own and had little or no knowledge of buying property.

Over the last fifteen years whilst building up my own substantial property portfolio, I have added a few twists and tricks to that approach on how to build a substantial property portfolio with no money of your own. I'm going to share it with you shortly.

The Long-term Potential of Property

Firstly, I know you probably have some doubts and concerns about buying or investing in property given the traumatic booms and busts we have seen in property markets historically—and especially over recent years—both in the UK and globally.

So let's get some facts straight and into real perspective.

- **Since 1957, property prices have risen on average 11.3% per year (source Land Registry).**
- **In the thirty years up to 2008, property values have doubled every 8.2 years.**

No other form of investment has shown that kind of return with such limited risk and the added benefit of leverage and gearing which I will cover later.

Sure, if you had bought into Microsoft when Bill Gates was still working in his garage you might have done a little better, but don't hold your breath waiting for the next one like that.

There are many factors that make property a very attractive, safe, and secure medium- and long-term investment in virtually any financial conditions.

> **MASTER YOUR MINDSET**
>
> Throughout history, the most reliable form of wealth accumulation has been property.

Ultimately everyone needs somewhere to live and the population is generally expanding. This, coupled with the rapid growth in divorce rates and in the numbers of broken families, means we will continue to need even more properties to house everyone.

Yet as environmental and other concerns put limits on development, available land in the areas people want to live is becoming scarce.

And while credit is not currently as easily available as it once was, many parts of the economy depend on a healthy property market.

The consistent growth in value over time makes property one of the best investments ever. When you buy a property in the right location and just hold on to it, you are very likely to make money—both through passive income and capital growth.

Of course, success in property is about buying the right property at the right price, but we'll cover that in more detail shortly.

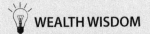

WEALTH WISDOM

Property has a long history of delivering high returns over the long-term.

The Attractions of UK Property Investment

Looking at the property market in the United Kingdom, for example, there has clearly been significant volatility in market values over recent years. Some of this was inevitable correction after a period of overheating due partly to easy availability of mortgages.

There are, however, many significant factors which suggest that in the longer term the UK property market is likely to remain fairly buoyant and would therefore be a very sound investment.

The obvious factor specific to the UK market is that it is a relatively small island nation with natural limits on the availability of land for building.

When you take into account the ever-growing population, combined with growing environmental concerns and the reluctance of many local authorities to give permission for further building, it seems highly likely that demand for existing houses and new properties will grow.

Added to that, the supply of council houses and other public housing is much lower than before. Over many years, there has been significant under-investment in building new properties which has led to a long-term imbalance between supply and demand, which shows no signs of improvement.

Even when demand for purchasing property is lower than normal, there are many factors that make property investment attractive.

On the one hand, there are more opportunities for bargain purchases. On the other, demand for rental property is higher and average rents therefore tend to be higher.

Clearly, it's very important to buy carefully in these market conditions but the most important factor is that the long-term outlook remains very positive.

Comparing Property with Other Investments

Just look at how property investment compares with the returns from other investment vehicles over the last ten years from 2001 to 2011, which takes into account the massive property slump after 2008. If you had invested £100,000 in each of the following investments over the last ten years, you would now have the following:

Stocks and shares	£100,000
Bank or building society	£125,000
Fine arts	£130,000
Single property	£193,000

That is what you'd get from owning just one property.

I'm going to show you how you could have turned the same investment into a portfolio of five properties worth £1.5 million in the same time.

But let's get there step-by-step.

How Your Property Grows in Value

Let's surmise that you bought a single property at a cost of £100,000.

We'll assume the property grows in value by an average of just 5% a year compounded, so the growth in the value of your property investment after each year will be as follows:

Investing £100,000 in a Single Property

Initial investment	£100,000
Year 1	£5,000
Year 2	£10,250
Year 3	£15,762
Year 4	£21,550
Year 5	£27,626
Year 10	£62,889
Added Wealth	**£6,000 a year**

So far so good. However, what if you knew where or how you could buy that £100,000 property for just £80,000? The compound growth you'd enjoy on that extra £20,000 is quite significant.

Bear with me, it is not that difficult to find and buy a property 20% lower than its true market value. I will explain how to do that shortly but let's stick with the example for now.

So, over those ten years, your property investment is delivering to you over £6,000 a year of added wealth. Does that sound good? Well it gets even better!

What if we take it up an extra level? Imagine someone showed you how to take your £100,000 investment and used it to buy *five* of these properties instead of one—with no extra out-of-pocket cost to you.

Again, please bear with me. I am going to explain how it is more than possible, but first let's follow through the example. Here is how the numbers from the growth in value would look now:

Investing £100,000 in Five Different Properties

Initial investment	£100,000
Year 1	£25,000
Year 2	£51,250
Year 3	£78,812
Year 4	£107,753
Year 5	£138,140
Year 10	£314,447
Added Wealth	**£31,000 a year**

Now you have around £30,000 a year of added wealth.

Getting interested? This time, for simplicity I didn't even add in the benefit of buying at a reduced price. This would make the returns even better!

The way we make this happen is through a financial tool called "gearing," which I'll explain shortly.

Gearing is simply a way to get greater leverage from the money you have available. It's achieved by using some of your money as a deposit and then borrowing more to enable you to make even more money.

Effectively you use the cash you have available as a deposit on several properties and then borrow the remainder of the costs with a mortgage to pay the balance of the purchase price.

Remember what we said about good debt and bad debt? When you borrow for gearing, that's *good* debt, because it *leverages* your assets to create more wealth.

As the properties you buy will be rented out, the rental income will not only cover all the mortgage costs of the borrowing it will also produce a monthly surplus which is *passive income*.

Gearing means you can end up in just a few short years with five properties worth £1,000,000 instead of one worth £200,000—all for no additional outlay or investment on your part.

The power of gearing means that a 5% annual increase in the property value is worth a lot more than 5% a year to you. The value of the whole property is increasing by 5% but remember you have only invested a small proportion of the total value—perhaps 10% or 15%.

The real return to you each year is therefore significantly more than 5%.

The exact rate of return will depend on a range of factors but historically, with the combination of gearing and leverage, annual returns of more than 8% a year have been achieved. There are many reasons to have confidence that such returns can be delivered in the future as well for educated investors.

That's why I happily used an 8% growth figure in some of the numbers we calculated earlier—such as the long-term costs of eating out and buying a daily coffee.

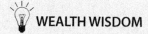

WEALTH WISDOM

Gearing allows you to make large returns from one relatively small down payment.

Adding the Power of Passive Income

The fact that these properties are rented out adds in one more factor—passive income—as this generates regular income for you and you don't have to go out to work for it at all.

Of course, you will have some costs to pay in running these properties—and for the borrowing costs—but buying the right properties at the right price should give you adequate surplus rental income.

If we assume you can make around £1,000 a month of surplus income from your five properties—after all borrowing and running costs—that gives you a passive income of around £12,000 a year.

So here is the result.

Investing £100,000 in creating a portfolio of five rental properties over 10 years at 5% a year growth would give you:

- £30,000 a year of added wealth through the capital growth—that is £300,000 profit.
- £12,000 a year of passive income through rentals—that is £120,000 in passive income over the same period.

Can you see the value in that?

In the next section, we'll cover the benefits of gearing in more detail.

 WEALTH WISDOM

Property provides the opportunity for very attractive passive income after all the costs of ownership have been covered.

The Property Wealth Wheel

I know you have a lot of questions so let me take you through the process step by step.

First I'd like to introduce you to the Property Wealth Wheel and the elements that make it up. Then I'll explain each part in more detail.

The six key parts of the process and the spokes of the Property Wealth Wheel are as follows:

1. **Psychology of Success:** To succeed in property investment, you first have to address the worries that put most people

off. This can include finding the right professional help and choosing to work with partners to improve the way you work.

2. **Profit Immediately:** You must buy at the right price which means you buy Below Market Value.

3. **Positive Cash Flow:** You want to buy property where rental income more than covers the cost of ownership.

4. **Popular Location:** Location is the key to buying the right property.

5. **Paying Creatively:** Financing your purchases in the right way enables you to buy more and pay less.

6. **Plan Your Portfolio:** You need to develop a strategy for creating a portfolio to achieve your specific objectives.

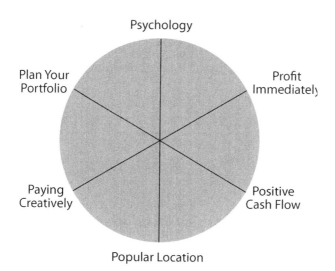

Now we'll look through these points step by step.

5

PROPERTY PROFIT SECRET 1:
PSYCHOLOGY OF SUCCESS

The first key to success in property investment is that you really have to start out with the right mindset. Many people never get beyond thinking about it because they have so many unresolved doubts, fears and concerns.

Here are some of the questions that typically arise when I am running seminars.

- Not knowing what or where to buy.
- Unsure if the numbers add up.
- Afraid of being unable to rent out the property.
- Concerned about management of the property—maintenance, problems with tenants etc.
- Worried about future increases in mortgage interest rates.
- Scared of possible major repair costs for the property.
- Put off by complications and costs about taxation.

I hope I'll address these concerns as we go through this section. Sometimes it's a question of getting the right advice before you make important decisions.

The key is that you have to approach property investment as a business. You must always buy with your head never with your heart. Put simply, as I'll explain in more detail shortly, that means you always want:

- Profit immediately by buying below market value.
- Positive cash flow by ensuring the rental income more than covers your costs and provides passive income.

Buying investment property is always a business transaction. It's never about how nice the place looks or whether you will get on with the neighbours. What you like is not necessarily what other people will rent.

You will most likely never live in this property yourself so it's always about the numbers and the figures stacking up correctly.

Doubts or fears are just based on a lack of knowledge and information and not having in place the right team of advisers whom you feel you can rely on and trust.

Therefore one of the key factors of having the right psychology is being ready to build the right professional team to support you. Another factor you may want to consider is partnering with others to get better results.

We'll cover these points in more detail later in this section.

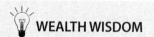

WEALTH WISDOM

People are often held back from investing in property because they don't have the right information about exactly what is involved.

5

SIX STEPS TO CREATING WEALTH AND PASSIVE INCOME FROM PROPERTY

PROPERTY PROFIT SECRET 2:
PROFIT IMMEDIATELY

One of the most important secrets of making money from property investment that professional investors know is that you must always make money when you *buy*.

Most people think you make money when you sell. But experienced investors understand that you make money when you buy—and even more money when you sell.

You really don't want to have to wait until you sell to make money.

This approach means that you will earn a much higher return on your investment and you make even more money when you sell.

The secret to making profit immediately is three letters: BMV. They stand for Below Market Value.

Let's look at an example of what this means in practice.

You decide to buy a property which has a market valuation of £385,000 and obtain a mortgage of 85% of this value—£327,250.

However, as your strategy is to buy below market value, you negotiate a discount of £74,000 on the true market value, meaning your actual purchase price is just £311,000.

There are two ways you profit immediately with this approach.

Immediate Equity

The first way you profit immediately is through the equity you own in the property right away. Your equity is the amount of the property valuation less the mortgage (£385,000—£327,250 = £57,750 equity).

Property Valuation	**£385,000**
Discount Negotiated	£74,000
BMV Purchase Price	£311,000
Mortgage (85% of valuation)	**£327,250**
Immediate Equity	**£57,750**

Immediate Cash

The second way you profit immediately is because there will be cash funds remaining from the mortgage amount after you have paid all the associated costs of purchase.

Mortgage	**£327,250**
	Associated Costs
BMV Purchase Price	(£311,000)
Property Taxes	(£11,550)
Legal Fees	(£1,000)
Broker Fee	(£1,700)
Total Associated Costs	**(£325,250)**
Post Completion Cash	**£2,000**

When you subtract the associated costs of buying the property (£325,250) from the mortgage (£327,250) you are left with post-completion surplus cash of £2,000.

Note that you may need to finance a deposit of 15% of the market value to secure the purchase before the mortgage is available. However, you will effectively receive all this money back when the deal is completed. This deposit can usually be financed by a bridging loan or similar method.

As a result of following this approach, you have an immediate equity stake in the property of £57,750 plus immediate post-completion funds of £2,000 after all the costs of purchase have been paid.

You can now begin to see how this strategy helps you build a substantial and valuable property portfolio without having access to huge funds of your own.

How to Buy Below Market Value

In order to buy for BMV, you will be buying from "motivated sellers"—people who need to sell fast. There are many reasons why people need to sell their property fast such as:

- Bank foreclosure and repossession
- Divorce or separation
- Relocation
- Death / Probate
- High renovation costs
- Old age
- Redundancy

It is not your business to worry about their problems. You have the opportunity to buy at a special price and this still provides a win-win scenario as you are helping them out of a problem.

Remember investing in property is a business and you must treat it as such.

Taking the emotion out of investing in property will serve you well and ensure you make good sound investments. If you always keep that in mind you will realise that, like anything else you buy at a genuine discount, it is just good business.

That is why there are so many opportunities to buy at a discount through the likes of eBay, Craigslist, Gum Tree, Cash Converters and Pawnbrokers to name just a few.

In every business and walk of life people need to raise funds and sell items quickly. Property is no different; the opportunities are just a little bigger.

You might think that finding people prepared to sell at below market value and in that situation is pretty rare and a matter of good luck.

However, such situations are happening every day and there are people and companies that specialize in identifying them and offering those properties to you.

There are several websites you can sign up to that give you this information or you can pay a specialist to track them for you.

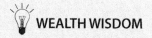

WEALTH WISDOM

You should focus on buying properties that deliver an immediate increase in value rather than having to wait for future growth.

5

SIX STEPS TO CREATING WEALTH AND PASSIVE INCOME FROM PROPERTY

PROPERTY PROFIT SECRET 3:
POSITIVE CASH FLOW

The next consideration is that you must always have positive cash flow from your investment property. That means your rental income must always be at least 25% greater than the mortgage payments.

For example, if your mortgage payment is £1,000 a month, you must have rental income of at least £1,250 a month.

This positive cash flow is how you generate **passive income**. The greater the difference between the rental income and the mortgage payments, the more passive income you generate.

Let's look at an example of the monthly costs and income based on a property valued at £200,000 with an 85% mortgage:

Monthly Rental Income	£1,100
Monthly Mortgage Payment	(£710)
Monthly Expenses and Running Costs	(£100)
SURPLUS MONTHLY RENTAL INCOME	**£290**

If you are aiming to generate high passive income, you need to identify properties where the rental income is much higher than the mortgage payment.

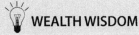 **WEALTH WISDOM**

You should buy properties where the rental income is more than enough to cover all the costs of ownership.

PROPERTY PROFIT SECRET 4:
POPULAR LOCATION

You have probably heard that cliché that the three most important factors in property purchase are location, location, location. However, it is no cliché. It is fact.

The location will always determine how good that investment property is going to be both for the short and long term.

A less appealing property in a great location will almost always do better than a great property in a poor location.

In order to find the best locations to buy, look for where some of the upmarket retail chains are located. They will always have done their research about the demographics of people in that area. Look for branches of Starbucks and smart cafes and restaurants. The target market of those sorts of businesses is yours too.

Here is something many people don't realise about successful retail businesses. Many of them derive more of their value from their property portfolios than from the actual trading results of their businesses.

Good locations are also going to be well connected, such as being within five or ten minutes' walk of transport links like trains and buses, or within five minutes' drive as long as there is good parking.

Other factors that make a location attractive are being close to town centre, shops, restaurants, and the beach.

They can also be in the catchment areas of good schools as people always want the best education for their children. Being close to good universities means there is always a demand for student accommodation.

Buying in a good location based on these criteria will almost always generate the highest passive income and capital appreciation.

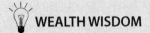

WEALTH WISDOM

It may be a cliché but it's true. Property investment is all about location, location, location.

PROPERTY PROFIT SECRET 5:
PAY CREATIVELY

People believe and think that you need money to make money. There is a misconception that you need to have a lot of liquid cash or access to large pool of savings.

While this may be true for the conventional property investor, it is certainly not true of a creative and well-informed investor. I have bought multiple properties without having to put any of my own money into the purchase.

The truth is you need to be creative to make money and the solution to that is the simple two-letter word GO!

That stands for the two most powerful wealth words in property investment:

- Gearing
- OPM (Opium!)

When it comes to making money from property, I just love Opium! It stands for Other People's Money!

Let's look at each of those in turn.

Gearing

Gearing is one of the key secrets to making money from property investment.

Let's say you have £100,000 in ready funds available to buy a property.

You can choose to use that money to buy a property for cash costing £100,000 if you wish. Clearly, if you follow the right strategies, you will be buying a property that's worth a bit more than that but the growth you enjoy will be on the £100,000.

Alternatively, you could use that £100,000 as a *deposit* and *borrow* some money so that you can buy a much bigger property. Remember, this will be *good* debt!

For example, if you use that money as a 20% deposit, you can buy a £500,000 property.

Purchase Price	£500,000
Deposit (20%)	£100,000
Loan (80%)	£400,000

In this case, we say your gearing—or loan—is 80%.

If you choose to borrow a higher percentage, you are said to be more highly geared. For example, if you choose to make a 10% deposit, you will have 90% gearing.

Let's look at the difference gearing could make to the returns you enjoy, depending on whether you choose to use gearing or not.

- Property A (No gearing): £100,000
- Property B (Gearing): Use the £100,000 as a 20% deposit on a £500,000 property

	Property A	Property B
Cash invested	£100,000	£100,000
Amount Borrowed	0	£400,000
Property Value	£100,000	£500,000

We'll assume each property grows in value by 10% a year.

The chart below shows how the two properties grow in value over several years.

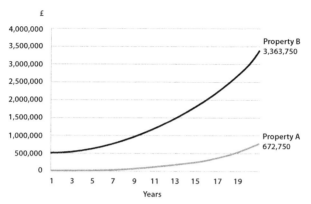

After 20 years, Property A is worth £672,750 but property B is worth £3,363,750. So you can see that using gearing to buy a much bigger property leaves you significantly better off:

- £644,000 better off after 5 years.
- £1,037,497 better off after 10 years.
- £1,671,000 better off after 15 years.
- £2,691,000 better off after 20 years.

The key to making gearing work most effectively is that you must be able to rent out the property and generate rental income that covers your mortgage payments and other expenses. That way, gearing gives you potential for enjoying very significant growth for no additional outlay on your part.

The higher your gearing, the greater your potential to share in growth. However, higher gearing also means higher borrowing costs and this can mean it is more difficult to cover your costs from the rental income.

This is one factor you will have to take into account in deciding the level of gearing you want to go for. Another factor will be that banks and finance companies will often require a minimum level of deposit of 10% or more.

The formula for working out how much gearing can increase the value of property you buy is called the Potential Property Purchase.

Potential Property Purchase = Deposit Amount / Deposit % (where the deposit percentage is expressed as a decimal).

For example, if you have a deposit of £100,000 available and plan to make the deposit 20%, your Potential Property Purchase is:
£100,000 / 0.20 = £500,000

On the other hand, if you want to make the deposit 15% of the total, your Potential Property Purchase is higher:
£100,000 / 0.15 = £666,667

Choosing only a 5% deposit would allow you to buy a £2,000,000 property.

OPM (Other People's Money)
The other way of building your property portfolio when you have limited funds available is to use what I call Opium—quite simply, Other People's Money.

This can be useful if you do not have funds available for a deposit or if you have a bad credit rating that stops you getting financing on terms that are attractive enough to you.

There are several ways of being able to create wealth from property without putting in your own funds.

Often it involves you putting in some sweat and leg work ("sweat equity") and then sharing the profit with someone who has the cash available but doesn't have the time, knowledge, or inclination to get involved in property investment.

For example:

- **Mortgage Hosting:** This is where you find a great property deal and arrange for someone else to take out the mortgage on it. You then agree with them an appropriate share for each of you of the surplus rental income and of the increased value when it comes time to sell.

- **Option Agreement:** This is where you find someone who cannot sell their property—typically they will not have much equity in the property. There are many people in that situation.

  You take a three- to ten-year option to purchase the property at today's agreed price. You will benefit from any equity increase during that period and any surplus rental income.

  When you follow the appropriate steps, this is a secure arrangement for both the seller and the person taking out the option.

- **Profit Share:** This is another approach where you find someone else to finance a property purchase and then plan to do a BRS—Buy, Refurbish, and Sell.

5

SIX STEPS TO CREATING WEALTH AND PASSIVE INCOME FROM PROPERTY

You do all the work in finding, renovating and then reselling the property while they provide the finance. You split the profit on an agreed basis.

These are just some of the options available that allow you to get involved in the profit potential of property investment if you don't yet have your own funds available.

The profits from these approaches may not be as appealing as when you are able to get the full benefits of gearing. However, one of these strategies may be a good first step in your property investment career.

And while the potential profits may be less than for full property investment with gearing, the benefits compare favourably with many other types of investments.

When with some other types of investment you might be lucky to get a 3% return on your money before tax, being able to earn a return of 10%, 15%, 20% or more is very appealing.

Property investment offers many strategies that give you the chance to make money without having money. You might be surprised how you can start to see results very quickly when you are willing to invest in your financial education and take action.

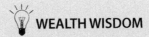

WEALTH WISDOM

There are many financing options that enable you to benefit from the growth of property values even when you don't have much cash available.

PROPERTY PROFIT SECRET 6:
PLAN YOUR PORTFOLIO

Before starting to build a property portfolio, you need to clearly define what you want to achieve as this will determine the actual properties you buy and what strategies you want to follow.

The two main goals you could focus on are:

- **Passive income**: This is the rental income the property generates for you after all costs. Once you have bought the property and rented it out, this income is paid to you wherever you are in the world.

- **Capital appreciation**: This is the money you make over time through the increase in the value of the property. For example, if you buy it for £100,000 and sell it a few years later for £190,000, it has appreciated by £90,000.

The distinction between passive income and capital appreciation is not an either/or choice. You may want some combination of the two but people, often depending on their age, tend to focus more on one than the other.

For example, younger people often focus on capital appreciation while older people concentrate more on passive income. Many others, including me, look for both. The key is to know where your focus is.

Deciding Your Objectives

So let's say you want to build a nest egg that will make you financially free and provides sufficient income to cover all your everyday living costs and expenses.

There is a simple formula that lets you work this out. If you assume you will earn 5% a year interest on your money, you need to multiply the income you want by twenty.

So, if you want an annual income of £40,000, the capital lump sum amount you would need is:

£40,000 x 20 = £800,000

If you assume you would earn 10% on your savings, then you would multiply by ten instead of twenty so you would need only £400,000.

Once you have identified the nest egg you want to create, you can devise a suitable plan to accomplish this.

There are various strategies you can follow to achieve different objectives, including:

- **Buy with low money down:** This could, for example, be an option where you use a lease arrangement to take over a property with an option to buy at some stage in the future. This gives you control for a low outlay and offers significant profit potential.

- **Buy with quick cash back:** This is where you make a purchase and look for an immediate return on the investment. This can also work extremely well using other people's money as you make a quick profit for low outlay.

- **Buy distressed sales:** These days there are many opportunities to buy property at very low prices when you know what you are looking for and know where to find them.

- **Buy, refurbish and rent:** You can buy a property that is in need of work and then refurbish it so that it becomes a high-quality rental investment.

- **Bespoke armchair investment:** If you have cash available or good credit potential but you have limited free time, you can work with others so that they do the work—which is their sweat equity—while you share in the profits.

- **Buy at discount:** This option allows you to get significant savings on the market value of properties for sale so that you can either sell quickly at a profit or hold for their rental potential. It can work for old and new properties. The key is being aware of these opportunities when they arise and knowing how to negotiate a good price.

The key with all these approaches is that the more you know about property investment, the more opportunities you have to make money, often using very little of your own money.

That's why I strongly recommend that one of the best investments you can make is in improving your own education about property investment.

213

> 💡 **WEALTH WISDOM**
>
> The more you know about property investment, the more chance you have to make money.

Professional Help

In order to succeed with property investment, you will need to build a team of reliable, professional contacts so that you have the right information and specialist knowledge.

You also have to decide if you are going to get a property specialist or mentor to create a portfolio for you, or whether you want to create one yourself.

Bear in mind that wealthy people make money by having the best people advise them and then continuing to work with those people to make them even more money. They use specialists to help them make more money and they are happy to pay.

If you want to make as much money as possible from your property portfolio, you need to build a strong team of expert advisers to help you make the right decisions at each stage.

Reading this book is an important first step. It is the strong foundation that you can build upon. As you develop your expertise, though, trying to economise by doing things yourself or by seeking cut-price help is a big mistake.

Having the right people to advise you will help you avoid the pitfalls, steer clear of bad decisions, save money and—most important of all—make bigger profits.

You'll need advice from some of these experts before you actually make your first purchase. Your expert team is split into two:

- **Professional advisers**: Help you buy the right properties in the best way to suit your needs.
- **Property specialists**: Help you make the most of your property investments by maintaining, developing and renting them.

Having the right team to turn to when you need advice and guidance is very important, especially if you're new to property investment.

The best way to find good advisers is to ask for recommendations from people who already have some experience in this area. Any recommendation that is not based on practical experience of working with someone is just the same as contacting a random name through Yellow Pages. The person needs to be checked out carefully.

Always see a recommendation as a starting point and not as evidence the person will be right for you.

The first group of advisers you need to choose are the professionals who will help you prepare what you need to do before you make your first purchase. They will then guide you through the necessary steps to build a profitable and effective portfolio.

This group includes your:

- Accountant: Especially for taxation matters.
- Solicitor: To handle contracts and purchase formalities.
- Mentor: Someone to advise you on property selection, purchasing and property wealth building.
- Mortgage broker or lender: Giving you access to sources of loan money.

What to Look for in an Adviser

Here are five things to bear in mind when choosing each adviser:

1. Specific expertise: Look for someone who has the right professional expertise in their field.

2. Property expertise: Make sure you find someone who has specialist knowledge of property investment.

3. Fees and service: Find out what fees they charge and how they work.

4. Property interest: Ideally find someone who personally owns investment properties.

5. Personal chemistry: You are going to share a lot of personal information, so choose someone you can trust and get on with.

You will also need a second group of advisers who will perform specific property tasks on your behalf as and when they are needed. Most of these won't be needed before you buy your first property but you will gradually build this team over time.

Some of the key specialists you'll need quickly are:

- A property manager who will manage your properties, ensuring you have rental income and your properties are looked after.
- Your property maintenance team or handyman to handle routine repairs and maintenance to your properties.

These advisers will make it much easier for you to build and manage your property portfolio.

Partner with Others

Finally you'll want to consider whether you want to team up with your partner, a friend, or someone else to help you.

I have two partners in building my property portfolio and I could never have achieved what I have done in property without them. We all bring different skills to the table.

You should seriously think about having a partner as this will help keep you motivated and on track and accountable to each other.

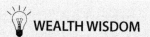 **WEALTH WISDOM**

One of the keys to success in property investment is surrounding yourself with the right professional advisers and partners.

LIFE STORIES: HOW SIMON BECAME A PROPERTY MILLIONAIRE

I began working with Simon when he was a thirty-seven-year-old divorced chiropractor.

He was in financial trouble due to his high levels of personal and business debt. These problems were combined with a reducing income as he was struggling to get clients.

We created a strategy that cleared all his debt in less than five years. During this period he invested time and money learning about property investments and even got involved in some small deals while still clearing his debts. That helped him learn that you don't need money to profit from property when you know how the system works.

- His first investment was a large flat in Nottingham that he bought at a distressed price from a couple who were getting divorced. A few small changes enabled him to let the property to six students.

- He then did a deal to buy a large house in Chester that had been repossessed and he had this split this into four apartments—selling two for immediate profit and keeping two for rental income.

- Using the power of gearing, he has now bought five more properties with a total personal investment less than £60,000.

The total market value of these properties is now over £1 million and he has passive income of around £5,000 per month after expenses.

His next target, which is more than achievable, is to take his property portfolio to a gross value of £5,000,000 within three years.

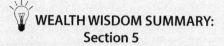

WEALTH WISDOM SUMMARY:
Section 5

- Property has a long history of delivering high returns over the long-term.

- Gearing allows you to make large returns from one relatively small down payment.

- Property provides the opportunity for very attractive passive income after all the costs of ownership have been covered.

- People are often held back from investing in property because they don't have the right information about exactly what is involved.

- You should focus on buying properties that deliver an immediate increase in value rather than having to wait for future growth.

- You should buy properties where the rental income is more than enough to cover all the costs of ownership.

- It may be a cliché but it's true. Property investment is all about location, location, location.

- There are many financing options that enable you to benefit from the growth of property values even when you don't have much cash available.

- The more you know about property investment, the more chance you have to make money.

- One of the keys to success in property investment is surrounding yourself with the right professional advisers and partners.

219

6

Six Secrets of Creating Extra Passive Income Streams

WHILE INVESTING IN PROPERTY is a great way to create an ongoing flow of passive income—as well as capital growth—there are other ways you can generate a steady stream of money in your life without having to continue working.

Wikipedia defines passive income as follows:

> "Income received on a regular basis with little effort required to maintain it."

This is quite a useful description as it highlights some of the important elements of passive income:

- **Regular:** You are looking for income that is delivered monthly or yearly in a steady flow. The actual amount may vary but the stream is continuous.

- **Little effort:** The income should continue on an ongoing basis with minimal effort from you. This is not about creating a new job that demands hours of your time. However, you may need to have some ongoing involvement which could range from a couple of hours a week to simply checking some paperwork every few months.

- **Maintain:** While you should have minimal ongoing commitment to keep the income flowing, you may need to invest time and/or money up front to create the income flow.

It can also be useful to make a distinction between *passive* income and *investment* or *portfolio* income.

Investment or portfolio income is where you receive a dividend or rent in exchange for an investment you have made. This counts as passive income as you normally have to do little or nothing to continue receiving this income.

If you are actively involved in managing a property portfolio, you may need to do a little more work. However this is generally quite limited unless you choose to do all the maintenance and repairs personally!

In some situations this distinction can be important as, for example, some tax regimes treat income from investments differently from passive income that results from your work.

Types of Passive Income

Here are some examples of sources of passive income:

- You develop a business model or a training program that you **license** to other people to use in exchange for a fee.

- You create a work such as a photograph, piece of music, or book that provides you with ongoing **royalty** income.

- You receive ongoing **commission** for something you sell once such as for the annual renewal of an insurance policy.

- You create an e-book or audio program that is sold for you online through **internet marketing** by affiliates and partners and you receive a share of all sales.

- You receive a **brokerage** payment as a share of ongoing sales for introducing people who do a business deal.

- You make a **venture capital** investment in a business with growth potential in exchange for a share of the revenues or profits.

- You receive a share of sales made by people in your **network marketing** downline.

- You invest in anything such as a car or a boat and receive **rental** income when others use it.

- You **publish** a series of online websites that give you affiliate or advertising income.

The principle behind all these types of passive income is that you make an initial investment—which may be money or time—and you receive an ongoing payment with little ongoing involvement required from you.

Leveraged Income

Although we are focused on passive income, many of the above examples could easily become substantial part-time or full-time jobs.

That's no problem if you are aware of what's involved and are happy to go down that route.

However, financial freedom is about being able to choose how you spend your time. And you don't have financial freedom if you are committed to spending several hours a day dealing with the issues of running a business.

Nevertheless, it may be worth committing to a limited period of highly focused work to generate a large amount of cash in a short time. We call this "leveraged" income as you can leverage a very large payment from a relatively small amount of work.

This can be very helpful for generating a large one-off sum which can either help you pay off debt or can be invested in property or other assets that will generate passive income in the future.

Some examples of generating a large payday from a focused period of activity include:

- Organising a major conference which generates significant income in ticket sales.
- Speaking at an event which leads to significant royalties or revenue from sales of your products.
- Creating a product and then selling the rights for it to someone else.
- Building a business and selling it quickly.

Although these may involve significant work on your part over a limited period, they can also generate substantial revenue that you can then invest to deliver passive income.

In his book *The 4-Hour Work Week*, Tim Ferriss talks about the growth in "mini-retirements." This is when people do not commit to long-term careers, but instead spend relatively short periods focused on projects that generate a lot of revenue.

They then take an extended break to enjoy the fruits of that success before moving on to something else.

So it's important to bear in mind that this type of passive income does not start out passive.

You have to make an initial investment of time and/or money which will later pay off by giving you some form of passive income.

 WEALTH WISDOM

An initial period of focused work can lead to a steady stream of passive income or a substantial profit that can be invested for the future.

Creating Your Own Passive Income Stream

In order to create your own passive income stream in this way, you need to create something that generates revenue.

In his book, Ferriss calls this a "muse." He defines that as an "automated vehicle for generating cash without consuming time."

This may sound a little too good to be true. But the rapid growth of the internet, development of new low-cost technology, and easy access to outsourcing makes this approach to earning money widely accessible.

Setting this up correctly is another way you can create financial freedom with a long-term source of regular revenue.

In this section, we'll look at the process you can follow to create your own streams of passive income.

The Passive Income Wealth Wheel

To help identify the steps required to make this approach work, I'd like to introduce the Passive Income Wealth Wheel. The six keys to this are:

1. **Psychology:** In the same way as the wrong mindset stops people from investing in property, people hold back from creating passive income steams because of doubts about their own ability or being uncomfortable about selling their skills.

2. **People with Problems:** In order to establish a profitable income stream you need to find a market ready to buy what you want. The people most likely to spend money have some problem they want to solve.

3. **Product:** You need to identify what you are actually going to sell. It could be a physical product, it could be an online product or it could be an idea you are going to license.

4. **Productivity:** In order to create a passive income, you have to set it up so that it runs on autopilot after you have done the initial work.

5. **Promotion:** You will need to create a strategy for how you are going to sell what you create.

6. **Profit:** You need to work out the numbers so that your work generates maximum profit on an ongoing basis for minimum work.

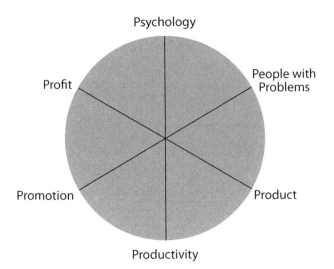

In the rest of this chapter, we will work through these aspects in more detail.

PASSIVE INCOME SECRET 1:
PSYCHOLOGY OF SUCCESS

Most people have skills, ideas, and knowledge they could turn into a significant passive income if they were ready to take the right steps.

However, most miss out on the opportunity because they don't have the right attitude and mindset to make money.

Here are some of the keys to developing the right mindset to build a passive income from your own expertise and ideas.

- **Believe in your own ability:** We usually get too close to our own knowledge and skills and don't easily see the potential to turn them into ways of making money.

- **Ready to grasp opportunities:** The difference between those who make money and the rest is usually more about being ready to take action than about having better ideas.

- **Willing to ask for money:** Too many people fail to make money from their skills because they don't value them highly enough. They often don't charge enough or even do things for free rather than asking for money.

- **Committed to promotion:** Many people with great ideas are waiting for the world to beat a path to their door. This is not going to happen and the only way to build an income stream in this way is to be willing to promote what you are offering.

- **Focused on success:** Many people who set out to make money in this way start out with the best of intentions but they fail to stay the course. The problem may be that they are put off when there is a problem or perhaps they are distracted by something that looks like it might be a better option.

There is a valuable concept that Robert Ringer talks about in his book *To Be or Not to Be Intimidated* called the "Leapfrog Theory."

The principle behind this is that as soon as you are willing to step forward with something you want to offer, you immediately leapfrog over the people who may have more skills but won't talk about it.

Of course you need to have something of value to offer—whether it is a product, service, book, or software package—but you don't need someone else's permission to step forward and take action.

Many people who have a great deal to offer hold themselves back and miss out on the opportunity for much higher income.

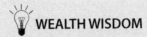

WEALTH WISDOM

If you want to generate passive income from your skills and ideas, you have to be willing to take action, implement your ideas and promote what you are offering.

PASSIVE INCOME SECRET 2:
PEOPLE WITH PROBLEMS

If you are going to offer a product or service that generates a passive income, you need to have a ready market of people able and willing to buy it.

You may be lucky in that you already have something to offer that has a ready market. However, for most people, the process has to start with some research to identify something they can offer.

- **What is the problem?** People will pay for solutions that give them something they want. Generally they will pay more money for something that solves a problem in their life. The bigger the problem, the more they are willing to pay. They will also pay for something that makes their life better somehow.

Essentially, people will spend on something they *want*, not necessarily something you think they *need*.

- **How can you help solve it?** Finding the problem may be the easiest part of the process. You need to come up with a solution that gives them a reason to spend money with you. For example, you may have to find a better way of delivering a service that is already available or develop a product that is more desirable.

- **Who suffers from this problem?** If you are going to make money from your solution, you need to be able to identify the kind of people who are likely to buy it. In most areas of business, trying to satisfy everyone means you end up satisfying no-one—so the more you can define your target market the better.

- **Where can you find them?** When you have defined your potential customers, you need to know how you are going to reach them so that you can tell them what you are offering. They may be in your neighbourhood so you can go and knock on their doors or they may be scattered all over the world so that you have to create a targeted advertising campaign to reach them.

- **How much money can you make?** A crucial part of the research phase is working out whether your idea is going to make you enough money. There is no point in solving problems that people will not pay to have solved or where the costs of production are higher than what people are willing to pay. It's therefore essential to ensure you take time to test the market before investing too much time and money in it.

If you are starting out in this process without a definite idea about what you are going to offer, you need to do some self-reflection to think where you are likely to have most success.

You are most likely to succeed with a product or service that leverages your own interests, skills, and experience.

Perhaps you need to start by thinking about what general area you want to create something in.

In his book *The Millionaire Messenger*, Brendon Burchard identifies the following six signpost questions to help you generate some ideas about how you could put your skills to good use:

1. The topics I have studied and been fascinated with in my life include...
2. The things I love to do in my life include...
3. Something I have always wanted to go out and learn more about is...
4. Things I have been through in my life that might inspire people or instruct them on how to live a good life or grow a good business include times like when I went through...
5. Based on these ideas, the topics I would love to gain expertise in and make a career helping others include...
6. The topic I would want to start with first and build a real career and business around is...

You need to research what people want and what is causing them problems.

Simply following traditional media such as TV, radio and newspapers helps you keep track of current trends. The news parts keep you up to date with what is important and the ads show you what people are currently buying and selling.

However there are many more specific places you can go for greater insight:

- **Online bookstores** like Amazon.com are a goldmine of data on what people are spending money on, for identifying trends and for finding out what people are looking for.

- **Online auction sites** such as eBay allow you to keep track of what people are buying in a wide range of markets. You will be able to see the most popular auctions and what people are searching for in many different topics.

- **Social media sites** like Twitter and Facebook can help you follow trends. There are sites in many specialist categories that can be particularly useful.

- **Online video sites** such as YouTube are a good way of finding out what people like spending their time doing.

- **Google and other search engines** will be one of your best sources of information. This will easily help you identify what topics people are seeking information on and how much competition there is. Most people only use a fraction of the valuable information that search engines provide. They give you a vast range of research resources including blog searches, book searches and video searches.

- **Online forums** provide venues where people with interest in a specific subject get together to discuss topics of common interest. The discussions give you a good idea of what common problems exist.

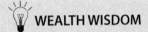

WEALTH WISDOM

In order to generate income, you must find a solution to a problem that an identifiable group of people are ready to pay for.

PASSIVE INCOME SECRET 3:
PRODUCT

When you have identified what people need, you have to find a way to deliver it to them that is convenient to them and profitable to you.

Remember this is all about generating passive income so you generally don't want to start setting up factories or shops.

There are many ways to deliver your solution but here are some examples:

- Book
- Software
- Home study course
- Physical product
- Forum or membership site
- Conference or seminar

Bear in mind that some of these will require more work to set up than others.

However the principle is that you should either be able to do the work once and enjoy passive income, or you should be able to do small bursts of work that produce a high return.

Bear in mind that there are several ways to make £100,000 in this way.

- Sell 1 person something for £100,000
- Sell 10 people something for £10,000
- Sell 100 people something for £1,000
- Sell 1,000 people something for £100
- Sell 10,000 people something for £10
- Sell 100,000 people something for £1

Generally speaking, the further up this tree you can be with your offer, the easier it will be to make money.

Product Creation

One of the factors you will need to take into account is whether you have the skills and expertise needed to create the product or whether you will need to hire others to do it for you.

You may not be a technology expert but if you have a good idea for some software that will solve a problem you know about, you can easily hire a programmer quite cheaply to create software for you.

For simple software the cost of development can be just a few hundred dollars or even less.

If you decide to deliver the software online, you have limited packaging and distribution costs.

You'll probably find that many popular and profitable products can be delivered online and therefore have very low production and distribution costs.

As an alternative, you can choose to set up a business that delivers physical products. You may find this offers less competition and suits your skills and needs better.

There are many ways to do this without running up high costs.

For example, if you design some unique jewellery, you could license it to another manufacturer or retailer in exchange for a share of the profits.

Or you could arrange manufacture yourself and limit sales to a few selected partners.

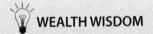

WEALTH WISDOM

Finding the right product to sell means establishing the best way to deliver your solution to your chosen market taking into account your skills, the needs of the market, and the profitability of production and distribution.

PASSIVE INCOME SECRET 4:
PRODUCTIVITY

The whole point of passive income is that you should have to do as little as possible on an ongoing basis to earn it.

Establishing the income stream may require some work up front but you need to set it up on the basis that this should not have to continue long-term.

The three keys to making this happen are:

1. **Automation:** One way to minimise your involvement is to automate as much as possible. For example, you can set up systems so that products are delivered online immediately after purchase. Buyers can then be enrolled instantly in a follow-up email sequence that works on autopilot.

2. **Outsourcing:** A simple principle of this approach to making money is that you should never do anything where someone else can do it cheaper and/or more effectively than you. There will be certain parts of the process that you will need to do such as making the decisions and guiding the strategy. You may also choose to do some things because of personal preference. For example, you can pay a ghostwriter to write a book for you but you may prefer to do that yourself. However, if you can pay someone less than £5 an hour to handle customer service issues for you, why would you do it yourself?

3. **Scalability:** Another way you can maximise your productivity is by creating systems that can be replicated and scaled. If you

6

find an approach that works for making 100 sales a day, you should be able to repeat the whole system to make 1,000 sales a day. You may do this by getting more customers or you could take the same idea into new niches and markets.

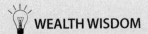

WEALTH WISDOM

In order to minimise your own time commitment, you want to automate and outsource as much as possible.

PASSIVE INCOME SECRET 5:
PROMOTION

If you want to create the largest possible revenue streams, you need to put your offer in front of as many potential customers as possible.

This means creating a promotional campaign to maximize sales.

Here are some of the strategies you can use for doing that:

- **Blog/website:** If you are going to deliver a product or service online, you will most likely need a blog or website presence to promote and deliver it.

- **Email marketing:** Even though people are increasingly swamped by email, it still proves to be one of the most effective ways of building contacts and making sales.

- **Social media:** Sites such as Facebook are becoming marketplaces in their own right where you can communicate with and sell to a wide range of markets.

- **Advertising and direct mail:** Targeted advertising and direct mail is still a highly cost effective way of reaching many markets.

- **Personal branding:** In many situations, you will need to take steps to build awareness of your own name to make sales. You can do this in many ways such as through writing, speaking and networking.

- **Pay Per Click:** Online advertising options such as Google AdWords are very effective both for testing your offer in the early stages and promoting it later.

- **Publicity:** Attracting publicity is a great low cost way of making people aware of what you are offering.

- **Video marketing:** Online video, especially YouTube, has become one of the most effective marketing and promotional channels for reaching many markets.

- **Personal selling:** In some cases, you will need to get out and sell face to face. This is particularly true if you are looking to build important relationships with key distributors or you have a physical product that people need to see.

- **Joint ventures and partnerships:** One of the best ways of reaching many markets—and of relying on others to make sales for you—is to create joint ventures with people who already have access to the customers you want. In exchange for a share of the profits, they will happily promote what you are offering.

The best promotional approach will depend on what you are offering and on your market. However it's clear that the more effective your marketing, the more money you can make.

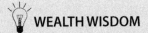

WEALTH WISDOM

One of the keys to the success of your offer will be getting it in front of as many potential customers as possible and persuading them to buy.

PASSIVE INCOME SECRET 6: PROFIT

The final key to your success in generating passive income is the amount of profit you make.

In some ways, this is the element that draws together all of the others.

Maximising profit is a combination of factors such as:

- Identifying the right target market.
- Finding a good solution that sells at the right price.
- Minimising your production and distribution costs.
- Maximising the effectiveness of your marketing.
- Scaling the delivery to make as many sales as possible.

Another aspect of profit is making sure that you set things up so that you reduce your own involvement in the operational side while still enjoying the full benefit of the income.

One of the big advantages of the development of technology and growth of the internet is that many approaches can be tested and developed with low initial outlay.

You can create something that you know is going to work before committing to it too much.

That makes this an ideal approach to generating large paydays and passive income streams.

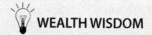 **WEALTH WISDOM**

Maximising profit is about finding a good market, making them the right offer and limiting your own involvement as much as possible while generating the highest possible long-term income.

6

SIX SECRETS OF CREATING EXTRA PASSIVE INCOME STREAMS

6

SIX SECRETS OF CREATING EXTRA PASSIVE INCOME STREAMS

LIFE STORIES: HOW MAGGIE MADE A FORTUNE FROM HER NEW-FOUND EXPERTISE

Maggie was a sixty-two-year-old grandmother who had always loved cooking for her family.

When her grandson was diagnosed with a condition that required a special diet, she spent time studying foods and recipes that would help.

She quickly discovered that many others suffered from the same condition but were not well catered for in recipe books or by food manufacturers. With encouragement from her son, she realised there were many ways she could help others in this situation while creating income for herself.

Over time she has become recognised as an expert in the field and has created several valuable revenue streams, including:

- Creating recipes that she has licensed to various food manufacturers in exchange for a royalty on sales.
- Developing an online video training programme that teaches parents how to cook and prepare the special food required.
- Writing a book of recipes and tips that became a top seller on Amazon.
- Running a recipe-of-the-month club online with hundreds of members.

While some of this required work upfront to get it established, she only spends three of four days a month working on this.

Most of the work is outsourced or automated. It still gives her a very nice income as well as making her feel good that she is helping others.

💡 WEALTH WISDOM SUMMARY:
Section 6

- An initial period of focused work can lead to a steady stream of passive income or a substantial profit that can be invested for the future.

- If you want to generate passive income from your skills and ideas, you have to be willing to take action, implement your ideas and promote what you are offering.

- In order to generate income, you must find a solution to a problem that an identifiable group of people are ready to pay for.

- Finding the right product to sell means establishing the best way to deliver your solution to your chosen market taking into account your skills, the market needs, and the profitability of production and distribution.

- In order to minimise your own time commitment, you want to automate and outsource as much as possible.

- One of the keys to the success of your offer will be getting it in front of as many potential customers as possible and persuading them to buy.

- Maximising profit is about finding a good market, making them the right offer and limiting your own involvement as much as possible while generating the highest possible long-term income.

Stepping Forward to Financial Freedom

I HOPE THIS BOOK has helped you see that, whatever your financial situation now, there are steps you can take to make it better.

No matter how deeply in debt you are, there is a way to turn the situation around and eliminate it much more quickly than you probably imagined.

Whatever your past record in saving money and building wealth, having access to the right information and taking control of your own financial future will enable you to get different results.

You can achieve a great deal just by following the strategies covered in this book.

When you make the changes I suggest to the way you think and behave in relation to money; when you follow the financial management approaches I outline, you can achieve a huge amount on your own.

Nevertheless, many people want a bit of additional help in various ways, for example:

- Access to more detailed information on key topics.
- Motivation and encouragement to take action.
- Helpful tools and resources to achieve results more easily.

To meet this demand, we provide a range of services including audio training programs, live events, and additional support resources.

In some areas, such as property investment, we offer highly personalized services such as consultancy and coaching.

The range of services we offer grows all the time so visit us at the address below and sign up for our free updates.

We are here to help you reach financial freedom as quickly as possible.

www.The6StepstoFinancialFreedom.com

Wealth   Wheel

Printed in Great Britain
by Amazon